Playing Life to Win

A GAME PLAN FOR SELF DEVELOPMENT

DR. TAYLOR HARTMAN

Author of THE PEOPLE CODE

For ordering or other information, please contact:
Novus, LLC
145 W Crystal Avenue
Salt Lake City, UT 84115
info@novusllc.us

n✶vus

ISBN 10: 1-934488-31-7
ISBN 13: 978-1-934488-31-7

Playing Life to Win

For TJ

Watching you swing away at life inspires me with tremendous hope for the next generation.

Acknowledgments

My work evolves from interacting with courageous people who are willing to face themselves. I fondly acknowledge all who have helped me learn about life by the difficult work you have done on yourselves.

My publisher, Lan England, always gives more than he takes and strives to give everyone the benefit of the doubt. Your innate personality and ethics make partnering with you both easy and enjoyable.

My editor, Lindsay Cahoon, observes in my writing what I can no longer see. Your clarity and competence make the work that I do much less painful.

My wife, Jean, lives the life I write about with such natural elegance. You remain my greatest inspiration in life for so many reasons and in so many ways. Thank you.

Contents

Preface

MY FATHER LOVED BASEBALL. He and my mother had seven children who lived (five died in childbirth). I think he was hoping for a complete roster to complete his own baseball team. He definitely would have liked that.

We grew up at 108 Roycroft in Belmont Shore, which has become a rather prestigious beach community in Long Beach, California. Not so in my childhood. Back then it was simply a place for middle class people to house themselves while they sorted out their lives. There was old Alf Gunn who lived across the street and played magic tricks while hitting us playfully with his cane. And the woman with a deep husky voice who lived down the street and dressed up as Santa Claus every Christmas. She sat outside her home in full costume for three weeks, giving gifts to every child who sat on her lap and yelling "Ho! Ho! Ho!" to every awestruck car that passed.

We lived one block from the beach, which seemed like our own private playground every day after school. I can't remember a holiday that all of us didn't go to the beach and draw our lines in the sand for whatever sports game we were going to play. My entire life was wrapped around sports.

I was the third of seven children—second boy! My sisters weren't much help. The oldest didn't want to mess up her "beehive" hairdo and the youngest was too plump and had limited vision. Ironically, my youngest sister became the most physically fit among all of us and her children are the most athletic. Go figure! Latent genetics I suppose.

For the boys, it was expected that we would play sports—any sport would do, but my father preferred baseball. We played it constantly, whether he was around or not. He loved the game and coached us all in Little League. I played water polo and tennis in high school, because it went without saying that each of my father's boys would play sports. Each one of us knew that anything less was unacceptable. And we played sports throughout our childhood because it was all we knew of life.

My father never tired of the game of baseball. Somewhere along the way I think he got lost between first and second base, but he never lost his passion for the sport. He simply understood the game and how it should be played. I remember going to the Anaheim Angels (now the Los Angeles Angels) games back when they lost more than they won. Watching my dad's intensity with every play was mesmerizing. He would yell at the players and curse the umpire. Listening to him was more fun than watching the game itself. The game of baseball never held the magic for me that it did for him. However, my life is much richer for having experienced baseball through his eyes.

When the Angels won the World Series in 2002, all I could imagine was my father, who passed away before he could see the day the Angels actually won, sitting on the Angel dugout with his baseball buddy, Don Criddle, rooting for his team in his afterlife. He wouldn't have missed the series. Not a chance! Not much meant more to my dad than playing the game of baseball the way it was supposed to be played.

I am sure that I was a disappointment to him in that regard.

Not that I didn't play the game; in fact, I even enjoyed it. But I was hardly the player he could have developed into a major league talent. I hit left handed and fielded with my right. I always batted second in the lineup because I could be useful if the first batter got on base by moving him around. One year I hit the game-winning home run in a Little League all-star game. He was our coach and I honestly thought he might pass out. Thinking back, he was undoubtedly more surprised than impressed, but it was good enough for me.

Actually it was more of a fluke than a genuine home run, but I did get to tag all the bases and score. With me up and batting left handed, all the fielders moved to their left because odds were that I would pull the ball to right field. As luck would have it, I hit a fair-paced grounder right over the third base bag—just fast enough for the third baseman to miss it and slow enough that the left fielder, who was clear out in left-center field, couldn't get to it before I flew around third base and headed home. Even now, when I reflect on that game, I am more pleased for my dad than myself. He loved the sport. Baseball never meant that much to me. Still doesn't to this day.

It means the world to my son-in-law Travis. After Arizona beat New York for the World Series in 2001, he lay back on the couch and said, "This is the best and worst day of my life!" Puzzled, I asked him "Why?" He answered, "Because I am so proud of Arizona and so bummed that baseball is over until next year!"

The passion that my dad and Travis—and many of you, for that matter—share for baseball intrigues me. You are not interested in only the final score but in every intricacy of how the game is played. You are fascinated with the various players' strengths and each team's limitations. You know the game's subtleties and have strong opinions on when a sacrifice bunt makes most sense and when to pull a pitcher who is in trouble. I, on the other hand, like the hot dogs.

My passion is people, and the lives people choose to live. I have strong opinions on when sacrificing oneself is legitimate and when it's time to hit away. I am fascinated by individual strengths and cultural limitations. I never tire of people and the difference they make in the game of life. Like winning in baseball, winning in life requires practice, dedication, and a winning strategy. In this book, I will outline the subtle strategies that are so critical to winning at life. I will teach you how to score by (1) seeing yourself for who you are, (2) facing powerful truths you prefer to ignore, (3) getting over yourself, and (4) making your life a legacy by getting others.

I hope you will enjoy my passion for a well-played life as much as I enjoyed my dad's pure love of baseball. In the end, I am a better person for what he taught me through the game of baseball, and I hope you will be a better person for what I share with you about playing the game of life to win.

Introduction

IF ONE IS to play a sport well, he must first understand the rules of engagement. Strategies, specially designed plays, and the overpaid all-star who's the envy of the sports world are all exciting parts of the game, but none exist without first establishing a solid foundation in the basics of the game. Getting the basics is the key to starting the game on a winning note. Like all sports, baseball has its own exciting elements. The home run, the double play, the runner who steals second, the pickle, even the hot dog-brandishing heckler who thinks he knows more about the game than the player (and isn't shy to tell him so)—they all make up the game that has become America's national pastime. Yet nothing crafts a truly well-played game like a firm grasp of the basics. To that point, let's lay down the foundation before we teach you how to score.

The first and most important thing to know about baseball is that the game starts and ends at home plate. The player—you in this analogy—steps up to bat at home plate. From the batter's box, the player must hit the ball to get on base and across home plate to score a run. In order to get back to home plate and score, he must tag each one of the bases (four in all, including home plate), without being tagged out by the opposing team. While one hit can get the player around the bases and back to home again, home runs are usually few and far between (even the best players hit only 40 to 50 home runs in an entire 162-game season), so every player needs his teammates in order to score. This truly makes baseball a team sport. No individual player can beat an entire team in this game.

While baseball is chock-full of intricate details and strategies, it is important to remember, especially for our analogy, that it is not the team who gets the most hits or the most players on base that wins. *It's the team who scores the most runs by the end of the game that wins!*

So, now that we've identified you as the batter, let's move on to how to play the game.

Your first goal when you get up to bat is to get a hit and get on base. In order to get on base, you have to face the pitcher and his array of pitches strategically thrown to get you to strike out. The analogy here is simple. The popular cliché "When life throws you a curve ball" comes to mind. In this book, the pitches we face while we're up to bat represent the varying experiences and events that life "throws" us. The good, the bad, and the sometimes ugly events of your life are all different pitches designed to keep you from getting on base. It is how you respond to those pitches that determines whether you get on base or not—you either hit the ball, get hit by the pitch, strike out, or walk. You cannot passively wait for four balls (a walk). You must swing at life's pitches. You must actively engage in life. Getting to first base is entirely up to you.

Once you've successfully reached first base, your focus shifts towards figuring out how you'll get around the bases and score by crossing home plate. In our metaphor, each base represents a fundamental step you must take in life in order to succeed.

Baseball scores rarely reach double digits; some of the most competitive games often end in a score of 1-0. This doesn't necessarily mean that either team isn't playing well, getting hits, and getting its players on base. It's simply difficult to score. Scoring in life is just as tough. Relatively few people actually win at life. They may get a few hits, but crossing home plate is an entirely different matter. To get home, you must learn to get others and make your life about them rather than yourself. And that makes all the difference.

More often than he scores, the runner, once on base, fails to make it around all the bases, remaining stuck on base when the third out ends the inning.

Truly great people (and teams) find ways to cross home plate before the inning ends. They refuse to live their lives stuck on base. In the game of life, you must first get on base and then emphatically refuse to remain stuck there.

To score in life you must:

1. Honestly see yourself as you are—strengths and limitations, hopes and fears, preferences and obstacles.
2. Face the truths about yourself and your life.
3. Get over your petty immaturities like pride, fear, and insecurity.
4. Learn how to make others successful.

To recap, I will use the following baseball terms indicative of life's terms:

- Baseball game = Game of life
- Batter = You
- Pitches = Circumstances of life and challenges
- Bases = Fundamental steps you must take in life in order to succeed
- Scoring = Creating meaningful relationships and helping others to succeed
- Dugout = Life support team

- Pickles = Difficult life situations you create because you ignore truth or can't get over yourself
- Swinging the bat = Playing to your strengths

The principles in this book will teach you what life's best hitters know about scoring and how you can successfully create a winning life.

Getting the Most from This Book

You don't have to know anything about baseball to get this book. In fact, you don't even have to like it. You just have to like the idea of improving yourself with the intent of making others successful.

Playing Life to Win is not simply about baseball. This experience is about discovering and utilizing the most important elements of life to your advantage, and baseball happens to fit well as a backdrop for my message. (However, you might feel the urge to eat a hot dog or snack on some peanuts while you read.)

Successful application of this book requires only that you be open to seeing yourself with new eyes. This book takes what scholars at Oxford University regard as the most revolutionary and correct personality theory in existence today—The Color Code—and uses its clarity to compose a complete guide to covering all your bases in creating a successful and rewarding life. And you don't even have to know how to read those confusing baseball hand signals to understand this book.

The truth is, life really is a game. It's a battle of wits, and those with the best strategies win. Unlike the game of baseball, however, few of us have the benefit of a seventh inning stretch or a long off-season to gather our thoughts, devise new strategies, and start again when the game resumes.

It's sad to see how relatively few of us take the time to stop and check how we're doing in the game of life. We simply endure and accept where our decisions take us, rather than assessing how we're doing and actually determining where we're going. Too often, we err in thinking there is simply no time to stop and reconsider our game plan. We are victims of our own wristwatches.

What's more, when we're in the middle of the game—living life at such a hurried pace—it can be quite difficult to see what we have become. Let's face it: we lie to ourselves. We get caught up in creating filters that excuse us from honest introspection. Filters can be gender-based (i.e. women can't lead or men don't have emotions). Filters are biases that we use to excuse our bad behavior, rather than see the picture accurately. We blind ourselves so we are able to sleep with ourselves at night.

Major businesses have failed because of this singular deception. Families have become dysfunctional—even destructive—due to collusion. Entire nations have lost their ways simply because they refused to see themselves for what they had become.

Chipping away at life's complex puzzle in order to see ourselves candidly, yet compassionately, for who we are and what our life has become frightening yet enlightening, painful yet ultimately freeing. Welcome to the game of your life.

FIRST BASE: GET YOURSELF

Understand and accept your natural strengths and limitations. Emotional Intelligence has been proven in research studies to be four times more critical to life success than IQ and technical abilities. Getting who you are and how you impact others is the foundation of self-awareness. Ask yourself when was the last time you received honest feedback from someone. How do you block important feedback from others? Are you playing to your personality strengths or limitations? What mechanisms have you put in place to help you see how you impact others?

SECOND BASE: GET TRUTH

Healthy people seek truth because avoiding it does nothing to free them from its consequences. In other words, refusing to face truth doesn't change the fact that it is truth. The truth will free you but will be initially more painful than taking the easier path of denial, rationalization, or justification. Getting to second base requires answering the following questions:

1. Are you 100% responsible for the relationships in your life?
2. Can you hear the truth about your choices and these consequences?
3. Do you have a built in system for confronting the brutal facts of your life?

THIRD BASE: GET OVER YOURSELF

This is my favorite base and the one that usually trips us up. We get stuck in our petty insecurities and allow our fear-based attitudes to hold us hostage. Selfishness is the number one reason that relationships fail both at work and home. What a tragedy when we settle for limited lives. Third base requires personal self-discipline. We must develop emotional muscle and become fit in order to lift ourselves and others to higher ground. Emotional maturity allows us to reach beyond our limited selves and see life through another's perspective. Getting over ourselves enables us to make life about others.

HOME PLATE: GET OTHERS

My favorite question to ask people is "Who loved you most effectively in your life?" Simply watching people reflect on this individual and the positive impact they had on another's life is inspiring. Who would miss you if you had not been a part of their life? Crossing home plate requires the gift of empathy. Are you a champion of customer service in both your personal and professional relationships? Can you legitimately connect with others in their language without inappropriately sacrificing yourself or the truth?

CONCLUSION

The ultimate goal for an abundant life is to help others be successful. To live this life you must become vulnerable and allow yourself to risk looking foolish. Becoming real is never easy and doesn't happen overnight. It takes a long time and doesn't happen when people are insecure and spend all their energy protecting themselves from the possibility of being hurt. To find what you were born to become means you have to leave the known and travel into the unknown. It means sharing your story with someone you care more about than simply protecting yourself. It is the essence of playing your life to win.

· · · · · · ·

This book is about life, using the backdrop of baseball.
It is a gift to you. Unwrap it.

· · · · · · ·

SECTION SUMMARY

Points to Remember
- When your life doesn't work, it is because you are stuck on one of the bases.
- At any given time, your life can be improved and you can start to score.

Questions to Consider
- Which of the four bases do you think will be the toughest for you to reach and why?
- Why is it so much easier for you to get to one base over another?

Application Exercise #1
Who are two people toward whom your behavior is more selfish than selfless?

1._____ 2._____

What are the consequences of your selfish behavior on the quality of your life?

1a._____ 2a._____

1b._____ 2b._____

Game Plan

DIRECTIONS: As you read each chapter, think of 3 specific actions you'll take to achieve these goals. Then follow your game plan!

SECOND BASE
Get Truth
How I will get truth:

1. _____
2. _____
3. _____

"A goal without a plan is just a wish."
– Antoine de Saint-Exupery

2nd BASE

3rd BASE

1st BASE

HOME BASE

THIRD BASE
Get Over Yourself
How I will get over myself:

1. _____
2. _____
3. _____

FIRST BASE
Get Yourself
How I will get myself:

1. _____
2. _____
3. _____

HOME BASE
Get Others
How I will get others:

1. _____
2. _____
3. _____

FIRST **1** BASE

Get Yourself

DISCOVER YOUR SIGNATURE SWING.

· · · · · · ·

MAKE LIFE PITCH TO YOU.

· · · · · · ·

STEP UP TO THE PLATE.

Chapter 1

Step 1: Discover Your Signature Swing

"The greatest thing a man can do in this world is to make the most possible out of what has been given him. This is success, and there is no other."

– ORISON SWETT MARDEN

OUR FIRST QUESTION in winning in the game of life must be, "How do I get on base?" In baseball, if you want to get in the game, you have to hit the ball. It's as simple as that. It's the most fundamental part of the game, yet everyone does it differently. Some choke up on the bat, while others prefer to bunt their way to first base. Either way, a player's signature swing is her trusted way to get a hit that will get her in the game and land her safely on base. It's comfortable and reliable because it's her way of hitting the ball, and no one else's.

Life isn't much different. Your signature swing in life is your trusted way of swinging at the pitches life throws you—it's how you live life on your own terms. *Your signature swing is your innate personality, the core of thoughts and feelings inside you that tells you how to conduct yourself.* As such, it is your own interpretation of life. What's more, it's built in—your personality came with you at birth. You did not inherit it from your parents nor is it a result of life experiences. It is you in the most basic and fundamental form. In other words, your personality is yours to use as you swing away at what life pitches you. You simply have to find out what it is.

Never the let the fear of striking out keep you from playing the game.

· · · · · · ·

"I always wanted to be somebody, but now I realize I should have been more specific."
– LILY TOMLIN

· · · · · · ·

KNOW THYSELF

At the height of the Greek Classical period, when society was much like today's, Socrates challenged the affluent and narcissistic masses who thought they knew all the answers with a pure and simple phrase: *"Know thyself."* This straight-forward but profound mandate has persisted to challenge us through the ages. Why? Because it really is difficult to "get ourselves"— to see ourselves for who we truly are!

· · · · · · ·

"It is only with the heart that one can see rightly."
– ANTOINE DE SAINT-EXUPERY

· · · · · · ·

It amazes me how much time and energy we waste ignoring ourselves. All too often, we exert all our effort just to get past who we are. We think that the only way to get ahead in life is to become someone we're not, ignoring our core personalities along the way. In doing so, we fail to see the power of our own signature swing—the effortless phenomenon that your own true personality brings to your life.

Many of us even try and explain away who we are by claiming it comes with our heritage. Nonsense. Two people with the exact same heritage are often noticeably different. Recent studies on twins have further manifested how uniquely different two people are even after developing in the same womb at the same time.

Consider John F. Kennedy Jr. and his older sister Caroline. Many historians have tried to explain away John-John's playful nature by connecting him to the "Kennedy mystique." If that were true, how do you explain Teddy Kennedy? Truth of the matter is that John, while deeply loyal to his heritage (and mother!), was a fun-loving, Yellow man trying to accent his life with the passion best expressed by the unique way he swung the bat at life. I can still see him rollerblading to work in downtown Manhattan as a young lawyer with a huge grin on his face.

. . . .

"Follow the grain in your own wood."
– HOWARD THURMAN

. . . .

People of the same personality orientation can appear very different from each other based on their upbringing and training, but at their very core you will always find the recurrent themes of who they were innately born to be. A great example of this concept is found in the late Mother Theresa and Madonna. Both Reds had the same driving core motivation in life—Power—and both marketed their causes remarkably well. The difference was Mother Theresa chose to use her power to serve the poor and the needy, while Madonna used hers in pioneering pop music and herself.

In this enlightened day in which we live, thousands of years after Socrates uttered his personality challenge, "Know thyself," it strikes me as very odd that so few of us have any idea who we *really* are. Many of us spend our entire lives spinning our wheels trying to get ahead in life and make something of ourselves, only to miss the key to it all—our unique personalities.

As a people, we have become so busy trying to fix what we do on a daily basis (our behavior) that we are often completely ignorant of the one factor that determines the success of our signature swing: *our core personalities with their driving core motivations.*

What does your signature swing *look* like? Describe it as others would. Do you see the same swing as they do? If you want to understand why you respond to life's situations in the way you do, you must look to the basic elements of who you are—what makes up your unique personality.

· · · · · · ·

"Know from whence you came. If you know whence you came, there are absolutely no limitations to where you can go."
– JAMES ARTHUR BALDWIN

· · · · · · ·

CHAPTER SUMMARY

Points to Remember
- You are born with your most natural gifts for getting a hit.
- To "know thyself," you must be true to your driving core motivation.
- Value the unique way you swing away at life.

Questions to Consider
- Are the adjectives you use both to describe yourself innately and to describe yourself currently similar or different?
- Which adjectives do you consider most positive or negative about yourself today? Why?
- If you played life solely by your innate strengths, would you consider yourself to be successful? Why/why not?

Application Exercise #1
List five adjectives you believe best describe how you would innately swing away at the pitches life threw at you as a child.

1._____
2._____
3._____
4._____
5._____

List five adjectives you believe best describe how you currently swing away at the pitches life throws you today. (May be similar to or different from your childhood adjectives.)

1._____

2._____

3._____

4._____

5._____

Application Exercise #2

Choose from both lists the five adjectives you believe are your best gifts for being successful in your life.

1._____

2._____

3._____

4._____

5._____

Chapter 2

Color-Coded Motives

FOR DECADES, PSYCHOLOGISTS, teachers, and parents have tried to explain who we are in the context of what we do, thinking that behavior somehow defines our very being. Frankly, they have it backwards—behavior is more often a reflection of personality rather than the other way around. In order to see yourself for who you really are, you must understand what drives you.

It can be tricky to understand what drives you, since life adds so many layers of experience to cloud your judgment of who you innately are. The key to understanding yourself at your very core comes in accurately identifying your core driving motives—which are your innermost reasons for why you think and act as you do. Your motives are also reflected in your needs and wants. Your motives determine why you do what you do, and therefore, stand at the heart of your unique personality. In other words, it is your *motives* that explain who you are, not your behavior.

. . . .

Motives are the basic hues that color our personalities.

. . . .

There are only four driving core motives that make up the numerous complex personalities in the world: **Power** (the drive to move from one point to another and achieve results); **Intimacy** (the drive for legitimate reciprocal relationships, sharing and connecting); **Peace** (clarity and calm in the midst of noise or troubled times); and **Fun** (the ability to embrace the moment and enjoy being fully engaged).

In my first book, *The People Code,* each one of these four motives is represented by a color. Each color comes equipped with its own set of characteristics, strengths, and limitations associated with its respective motive. *(Incidentally, when I refer to a person as being a particular color, I am not making a reference to race or color of skin. Each of us should be color blind in that regard.)*

When we honestly evaluate ourselves, each of us ultimately identifies most closely with only one of the four personality colors. Do not confuse your core personality with your personal history. We all have personal histories that reflect our different individual life stories. We create our personal histories from a variety of sources, for example, the effects of different life events, societal norms, birth order, race, religion, and personal choices. Of course our personal histories influence the people we have become today. However, our personal histories are not our core personalities. Our core personalities reflect how and why we responded to the life events, societal norms, birth order, race, religion, and personal choices in the way we did. We must always look beyond our life experiences to see our innate, natural, driving core personalities, which we brought with us at birth.

Reds are driven by Power, or the need to be able to get things done. If you are a Red, you are determined to move from point A to point B in life as quickly and efficiently as possible. Closely related to Power is your innate desire for leadership. You enjoy being in the driver's seat and prefer life on your terms. As a Red, you are also extremely productive—whether in school, at work, or in your personal relationships. You enjoy being anxiously engaged in the causes that you deem worthwhile and seek approval only from people you respect. In fact, being respected often resonates more comfortably with you than even being loved. You are logical and practical in all that you do and typically state the facts as you see them.

Blues are driven by Intimacy, or the need for emotional connection. If you are a Blue, then more than anything else, your life must have purpose. A true Blue will sacrifice a successful career in order to improve an important personal relationship if necessary. You are altruistic and seek opportunities to enhance others' lives. You also seek to please others. The strings you often attach to your many generous gifts are that, in turn, you be understood and appreciated for your efforts. Blues usually expend great effort in making the world a better place and feel directed by a strong moral conscience. You value appropriate behavior and need constant assurance that you are legitimate, cared for, and well thought of by others.

Whites are driven by Peace, or harmony within—oneness. Peace does not mean to be in a place where there is no noise, trouble, or hard work; rather, it means being calm in one's heart, even in the midst of those things. Kindness to others comes very easily to you and your quiet reflection offers up remarkable clarity for anyone willing to ask your opinion. You are not inclined to offer suggestions without specific solicitation. You see life rather objectively, and you comfortably embrace individuality in yourself and others. You flow through life patiently and without ego, trusting the old Chinese adage that "all things eventually come to he who waits." Internal motivation, external confrontation, and articulation of inner thoughts are most likely your natural Achilles' heel. It is uncommon for others to find you difficult to be with, but equally rare to find someone who knows your inner fears, hopes, and true expectations in life.

Yellows are driven by Fun. If you are a core Yellow, you consider life to be a party that you're hosting. You enthusiastically embrace life on all fronts and generate extraordinary optimism when facing life's problems. You live in the moment and invite everyone who is positive to join you. Lady luck feels at home riding on your shoulder and people often seek your company. You welcome the spotlight and opportunities to perform, and often ignore legitimate criticism and/or important life details that seem routine and ordinary. You are highly adventurous and are always ready and willing to spontaneously jump at the next life adventure placed before you (as long as someone else does the planning!). You epitomize the race horse as opposed to the plow horse and typically have a nose for shortcuts.

As Socrates challenged his peers to know themselves, I challenge you to know yourself in color. Accurately identifying your core personality facilitates your ability to play to your strengths and see yourself for who you really are inside, underneath the countless ensembles of clothes your own life experiences have layered you with! In other words, if you're truly a Red at heart, but life's experiences have led you to behave as a White, then your first step in getting to first base is to see yourself as you truly are. Get back to being a good Red.

Color coding helps you understand why you react the way you do—it gives you a solid foundation from which to work in making sense of the countless facets of your behavior. *The People Code* provides a complete picture of who you are at your innermost self! After all, would you rather piece together a 500-piece jigsaw puzzle with or without an accurate rendition of the completed picture in front of you?

Once you see yourself in color, *your personality* becomes uniquely yours—something for which you, and only you, have complete and sole responsibility to value, embrace, and express. It becomes your own "brand" for approaching life's myriad of events. It is not a collection of genetic traits or inherited qualities passed down from generation to generation. It is something you brought with you when you came into this life—it is yours alone with which to swing away at life. It is what initially differentiates you from everyone else. It is *your signature swing.*

CHAPTER SUMMARY

Points to Remember

• Your signature swing in life is your trusted way of swinging at the pitches life throws you—it's how you live life on *your own terms.*

• You are driven by one of four driving core motives: Power, Intimacy, Peace or Fun.

• Your personality it uniquely yours, differentiating you from everyone else—it is yours alone with which to swing away at life. Use it!

Questions to Consider

• Does your innate personality align well with how you live your daily life?

• Did your parents value you in your innate core color?

• Has your personal history enhanced or detracted from your innate core personality?

• What positive traits have people most often praised you for?

• Of all your natural gifts for swinging at life's pitches, which are you proud you have?

Application Exercise #1

Go to www.thecolorcode.com and take the free Color Code Personality Test. Compare the results of your online profile with the adjectives you used when assessing yourself in the last chapter.

Application Exercise #2

Stand on one leg. Then stand on your other leg. Which one is easier? The leg that is easier to stand on represents your core personality. Each one of us has a natural personality preference just as we prefer standing on one leg better than the other.

Chapter 3

Step 2: Value Yourself

"To be yourself in a world that is constantly trying to make you something else is the greatest accomplishment."
- RALPH WALDO EMERSON

MANY FORCES ENDANGER our innate personalities from ever seeing the light of day. Sometimes we learn early in our young lives to reject our gifts because someone we trust rejects us. Such rejection creates negative biases that may attack our innate validity and cause us to resist fully embracing who we are, thus severely hampering our success in life. These biases may come from family, culture, or religion—the very forces that often act in our favor when they are healthy and legitimate. The scars resulting from these biases can take years to remedy before they are completely resolved.

Illegitimate biases will lie to you about who you were innately born to be and what you were born to do with your personality. Remember, you come bearing wonderful, unique, important gifts, which you must discover and incorporate into who you are and how you interact with the world around you.

The best players see themselves accurately. They know their

preferences, strengths, and limitations. They know what they bring to the game and what they need from others in order to win. *The best players value themselves for what they are and what they are not!* Once they are clear about their strengths and limitations, they commit to developing themselves—playing to their strengths and seeking "coaches" who can help them overcome their limitations. They seek honest feedback and do their work in getting to know themselves well enough to know what needs fixing.

* * * * * * *

Life's best hitters and most successful teams in business and in sports are committed to an internal and ongoing process of personal development and change.

* * * * * * *

It is not always the person who *appears* to be the most valuable on a team or in life, who actually is! Unfortunately, our society does not always value personalities or principles that equate to being healthy or legitimate (think being thin and eating disorders). Surely anyone who attended high school understands how petty biases can skew reality. Sometimes being true to yourself flies in the face of how society wants you to be. Unfortunately, many of us succumb to societal pressures and abandon our signature swings for something that appears more superficially attractive or popular. The consequence ultimately leaves us without legitimacy or genuine self-respect.

Once I shared the podium with a well-known southern California news anchor. As our host introduced us to each other, she mentioned to the celebrity newscaster that once she heard me speak she would never see herself or others in the same way again. Instead of intrigue, the newscaster offered disdain—how absurd to even consider that she might want or need to change how she viewed herself or others. "Why would I want to change how I see myself?!" she demanded, "My friends and I like me just the way I am!" Afraid to be seen by society as unacceptable, she refused to value her true self and worked tirelessly to impose her façade on the world.

This newscaster's arrogant behavior was simply a mask for deep-rooted insecurity that came from a lifetime of hiding. Throughout her speech to the audience, she bragged about clawing her way to the top, having no choice but to leave dead bodies along the way. Society's Cinderella was nothing more than an ugly step-sister in fear of being exposed. After all, if society couldn't value her in the image she projected, surely she could never come to value herself for who she really was.

Her fear of being exposed screamed out in defensive reactionary behaviors. Not only did she refuse to value herself, but she had long forgotten who she once was. Who knows why? For many of us, negative biases attack early, encouraging us to lie to ourselves and deviate from our legitimate personalities.

Her entire sense of self was based on how others perceived her rather than the simple truth of who she innately was. She had turned herself over to public applause much as we all do when we defer to our careers, families, peers or other life forces out of fear—a strategy that will never get us on first base. This newscaster had become so out of touch with herself that her entire speech was riddled with excuses for her hostile and inappropriate behavior. While she had duped herself into believing she was hitting homeruns, she was actually still at the plate, whiffing at fast balls.

• • • • • • •

"Oh what a tangled web we weave, when first we practice to deceive."
— Sir Walter Scott

• • • • • • •

PARADOX OF SELF-AWARENESS

Typically, the difference between someone who gets a hit and someone who is constantly sent back to the dugout is *emotional security.* Hitters are secure enough to see themselves for who they are, while dugout-dwellers are so unsure of themselves that they try to become someone and something they're not—they go against the grain of their innate personalities.

• • • • • • •

The more secure people are, the more likely they are to see
themselves accurately—the more likely they are to get a hit.

• • • • • • •

This is what I call the "paradox of self-awareness." Those who are willing see themselves honestly, seem to invite candid feedback and adjust themselves accordingly. Their very nature increases the likelihood that they'll improve as they go through life. On the other hand, insecure people resist and reject the very feedback that could save them from themselves. So desperately fear-driven, they stubbornly argue that they are who they want to be. Over time, their lies become bolder and they slide further and further from the truth about themselves. Lives that could be so abundant in the light of truth shrivel in scope, often leaving a limited legacy.

This insecurity is akin to the age-old fable about the four blind men who attempt to describe an elephant using only their sense of touch. As the story goes, the four accurately described the section of the elephant that each could individually feel—the wet trunk, the large round belly, the short stringy tail, the stumpy legs—but were limited to only that section of the elephant. While each correctly described the part of the elephant he could touch, none had the benefit of seeing the whole picture, and thus, remained limited and incorrect in his description of the elephant.

Tragically, some of the most famous and wealthy individuals in the world suffer from this type of blindness. They are terribly insecure and often feel a sense of personal inadequacy, which acts as a blindfold and limits them to describing only the part of themselves they can comfortably feel and value. Insecure people often work the hardest to compensate for their insecurities by becoming "successful" and "over achievers" so others won't see them as they fear they might be. It becomes a self-fulfilling and limiting process. The more successful and accomplished they become, the less feedback they receive and the better able they are at hiding from themselves and others.

The secret to the paradox of self-awareness lies in assessing yourself on three crucial queries:

1. The things I know that I know.
2. The things I know that I don't know.
3. The things I don't know that I don't know.

The third one is where we most often get into trouble! *What we don't know that we don't know about ourselves can be severely debilitating.* How do we discover what we don't even know exists? This is where playing on a team makes a huge difference. Others see what we can't; invite their insights. Ask them about how they see you swinging away at life.

Recently I worked with a team of young executives. I asked them to complete the Hartman Character Profile, which highlights current individual strengths and limitations. It actually became rather comical to those of us with some wear and tear under our belts (older guys) as to how much they did not know they did not know about themselves. They gave themselves surprisingly high marks across all colors in the strengths and surprisingly few marks across all colors in the limitations. They were as yet unaware of themselves and how they impacted others.

It's your life. But the entire team is affected by whether or not you get a hit. So, how you swing at life affects everyone. Unless you cross home plate, they lose too! And if you can't get to first base, you haven't got a prayer of crossing home plate!

· · · · · · · ·

"Only by much searching and mining are gold and diamonds obtained, and man can find every truth connected with his being if he will dig deep into the mine of his soul."
– JAMES ALLEN

· · · · · · · ·

CHAPTER SUMMARY

Points to Remember
- The best players see themselves accurately. They value themselves for what they are and what they are not!
- You have work to do on yourself. Find out what it is and commit to doing it.
- The paradox of self-awareness is that those individuals who are most self-aware are also the same ones who invite feedback while those who are least self-aware reject feedback about themselves.

Questions to Consider
- How often do you get honest feedback about yourself?
- Who is your most candid contributor about how you impact others?
- How do you restrict others from nurturing your self-awareness?

Application Exercise #1
List three people you trust to give you candid feedback about you. Ask them to share the two most positive ways you impact others and one thing about you they wish you would change that currently inhibits your effectiveness. Transfer these responses to a card and review them daily until you receive an unsolicited compliment on your improvement.

Name: _____

Improvement: _____

Strength 1) _____

Strength 2) _____

Name: _____

Improvement: _____

Strength 1) _____

Strength 2) _____

Name: _____

Improvement: _____

Strength 1) _____

Strength 2) _____

Chapter 4

Who's In Your Dugout?

THE DUGOUT IS where you find solace with your team. Whether you've just been sent back to the dugout after striking out or you are coming in after scoring a run, you can count on your best supporters waiting for you in the dugout. They cheer your successes as openly as they help you get over your shortcomings.

. . . .

"The strength of the team is each individual member; the strength of each member is the team."
– COACH PHIL JACKSON

. . . .

A strong dugout makes valuing yourself considerably easier. Surround yourself with people whom you trust, people who will provide you with candor on how you're playing the game. Hopefully your dugout is filled with co-workers, close friends,

and family. Whether they personally have the skill you're seeking to develop or not, chances are they can see your performance from the dugout better than you can see yourself while
you're up to bat. Remember, there's no mirror next to home
plate. Ask them for feedback and constructive criticism and be
willing to hear what they have to say.

In his wildly successful first season with the television show
The Apprentice, corporate mogul Donald Trump illustrated the
importance of surrounding yourself with a strong support system. "Dog does not eat dog," he declared to his young participants vying for a leadership position in his company. To his
point, they could not succeed without a strong support system
in their lives. Neither can you. There is a reason a baseball team
has nine players actively playing at the same time. No one can
play the game alone.

· · · · · · · ·

**Only half the major league players ever hit
a homerun in their entire careers!**

· · · · · · · ·

Ironically, insecure people rarely seek help from anyone else.
They think they can figure it out on their own but find themselves sadly disappointed. Without help from others, we struggle to improve our game by overcompensating for our inade-
quacies without coming to terms with them. Insecure people
never cross home plate consistently enough to win at life. They
never see themselves honestly enough to win the game.

The humble player welcomes and even openly seeks help in
improving himself. In his quest for legitimacy, or being true to
who he really is, the humble player is unafraid to reveal his lim-

itations. When my son, TJ, was twelve years old, he asked me to help him overcome his innate shyness. He suggested that perhaps he should answer the front door when adults stopped by in order to learn to look them in the eye and say "hello". His humility and support from the dugout freed him to develop a social confidence. Today, no one would ever guess that TJ was once very shy (except that his big-mouth father has now told the entire world!).

CHAPTER SUMMARY

Points to Remember
- You must develop a strong support team in order to win in life.
- Once you identify your strengths and limitations, commit to developing yourself.
- Surround yourself with people you trust, people who will provide you with candor on how you're playing the game.

Questions to Consider
- What criterion do you use for placing people in your dugout?
- Have you ever changed the people in your dugout and seen improvement in your life?
- Is there someone who used to be in your dugout that you should invite back in?

Application Exercise #1

List the nine most critical players in your dugout today:

1) _____ 2) _____
3) _____ 4) _____
5) _____ 6) _____
7) _____ 8) _____
9) _____

- Star the ones you solicit feedback from most often.
- Ask yourself who you need to seek help from right now. Why?
- Commit to replacing unsupportive teammates with legitimate players on your life's roster A.S.A.P.

ıter 5

p Up to the Plate

"We must be the change we wish to see in the world."
– GANDHI

ONE OF MY favorite phrases in baseball is "Step up to the plate!" It's short and simple, yet no other phrase in baseball is as powerful. It connotes taking responsibility and living up to your expectations. The image of the orphan boy Pip in Charles Dickens's masterful work *Great Expectations* comes to mind. When this previously insignificant child, deemed worthless by those around him, receives an inordinate inheritance from an unknown benefactor, the theme of his life centers around his newfound wealth and what he will do to live up to the lofty expectations created by such a gift. With so much riding on what you've been given, the gift of your own life and person-ality, how are you going to respond? In the Dickens classic, Pip vowed to make something of himself, to lift himself out of the ruins of his young life. How will you respond to your unique gift of personality? When all is said and done, it's your life. How will you step up to the plate and own what has always been yours to fulfill?

· · · · · · ·

We live in a victim society that emphasizes personal rights over personal responsibility.

· · · · · · ·

100% RESPONSIBILITY

Perhaps one of the most basic (and most often ignored) principles in life is to take full responsibility for who you are. We can't expect to hit the pitches life sends our way until we do. Rich or poor, white or black, old or young, God-fearing or atheist…we all have the responsibility to own our life. Mohandas Karamchand Gandhi, a great citizen of this world, is perhaps best remembered for leading millions of his countrymen in India to independence from one of the greatest empires in history without the use of violence. Gandhi's life and teachings reflect a very different orientation than making lots of noise about personal rights. He focused entirely on becoming *personally responsible* versus demanding personal rights!

We must take responsibility for the lives we lead. Accepting the natural rewards and consequences for our actions not only makes life easier, but such humility enables us to grow and mature. (More on this in Chapter 11 on second base.)

100% RESPONSIBILITY CLUB

When was the last time you accepted full responsibility for a problem in your life? When was the last time you heard anyone say, "That's completely my fault. I am 100% responsible for what happened and will do whatever is necessary to make it right!" When did taking 100% responsibility for your thoughts and actions become the exception rather than the rule?

We have created a society of victims with a cultural backdrop that actually promotes blame, denial, and rationalization rather than responsibility and ownership. Today, if you smoke three packs of cigarettes a day for forty years and die of lung cancer, your family blames the tobacco company. If your child misbehaves in school, you give him the label ADHD and medicate him. If your neighbor crashes into a tree while driving home after too many drinks at the bar, he blames the bartender.

Have you noticed how rarely anyone steps forward to take ownership for creating the problem when something goes wrong today? Even more rare is the individual who takes 100% responsibility for creating the problem *and* accepts ownership for providing a solution. Those individuals and/or companies who pay their membership dues by exposing their vulnerability ("It was my fault!") and accept ownership for resolving the problem ("How can I make it right with you?") earn the privilege of becoming exclusive members of the 100% Responsibility Club. Trust me, this club is highly exclusive and holds its members in strict adherence to principles that far exceed the general public's expectations.

The 100% Responsibility Club has members from all around the world. One of the club's founding fathers in its North American Franchise was General Robert E. Lee. He is still regarded as the most beloved general to serve in the American military. As we read in Michael Shaara's *The Killer Angels*

(Ballantine Books, 1987), after the pivotal battle in the American Civil War at Gettysburg, General Lee asked to be relieved of his command. Of the battle he said, "No blame can be attached to the army for its failure to accomplish what was projected by me. . . . I alone am to blame, in perhaps, expecting too much of its prowess and valor . . . could I have foreseen that the attack on the last day would fail, I should certainly have tried some other course . . . but I do not know what better course I could have pursued."

Could you describe the disappointments in your life as respectfully as General Robert E. Lee did on numerous occasions throughout both his personal life and professional career? Members of this elite club can. As with all true principles, the rewards far outweigh the dues. Yet few of us are willing to pay our dues, simply because we lack the emotional intelligence to do so.

Compare two recent experiences I had with major companies. The first displayed no responsibility and the second assumed full responsibility. Guess who gets my future business?

A Rental Car Company

I think their slogan used to be "We try harder." Not anymore—or at least not at the Orange County Airport. I arrived very late at night with luggage in tow. I went directly to the rental counter in the parking structure, some distance from the arrival gate at the airport. There was not another soul for miles—just the rental agent and me.

He informed me that I must return to the upstairs counter in order to get my car because he could not process my paperwork. Seasoned business traveler that I am, I informed him that it seemed a rather arduous and unnecessary task at this very late hour. My flight had already been delayed and I had hoped to get to my hotel by midnight. He sighed deeply—clearly perturbed by my insistence that he accommodate me.

"Perhaps I will do you the favor of making this onetime exception," he said. "Thanks" was all I could muster, knowing full well that it would be the only exception he'd ever have the chance to make for me because I would never rent from this company again. His deep sigh, dismissing any responsibility for helping resolve the problem pleasantly was quite pricey considering how often I rent vehicles.

Marriott

Same week, different town. I was in New York City at the Renaissance Marriott Hotel. I was staying there expressly because I had been told how this hotel beat out Marriott for the annual NYC Customer Service Award and was subsequently purchased by Marriott under the adage, "If you can't beat them, buy them." Staying with them was not a great experience. I relocated rooms once because of the noise from being too close to the elevator (shame on me!) and wasted 2 hours and $35 on cab fare headed the wrong direction due to the concierge's error in writing the wrong address. But, not altogether a bad experience.

Upon checking out, the receptionist asked about my stay. "It was okay" were my exact words. She looked me straight in the eye and said, "How could we have made your stay with us better, Dr. Hartman?" I told her. She offered some form of compensation. I declined. She offered again. Again, I declined and said that I should have complained about the specific problems I had encountered to the appropriate person at the time. She pressed me once again: "I won't feel right about our relationship until I can be assured the same experience won't happen again." I assured her that she already had and that I would definitely be back.

The rental car agent was concerned only with completing a transaction. The Marriott receptionist focused on building a relationship. Quality relationships require 100% responsibility. The ability to take 100% responsibility requires valuing yourself (your product, your service) so much that you can afford to be wrong, make mistakes, be vulnerable, make amends, and still affirm your value to the party who feels wronged or offended. It requires a true leap of faith that by taking 100% responsibility for the relationship and doing right by others in every situation, you free yourself to succeed.

Talk about swimming upstream! Nothing is more counter to our current victim culture of making excuses for ourselves and blaming others than the theory of taking 100% responsibility for your relationships. First let me explain "what generally is" and then move to "what specifically can be." What is the current culture? What does it look like? Why do you embrace it? And most importantly, why doesn't this culture work?

THE STATE OF "WHAT GENERALLY IS"

Unfortunately, many of us have been raised in a victim society. We have been taught by countless role models that our problems are not our own doing and that we, in fact, have been wronged. For many reasons (misunderstood, abandoned, and neglected all come to mind), we have spent more energy seeking strategies for "getting off the hook" than facing the music when we make mistakes.

Think President Bill Clinton and Monica Lewinsky. Think of most partners during divorce proceedings. Think of driving while under the influence, Enron, public education, and major airlines. We have been taught and learned our lessons well.

Most of us were very willing students. We excuse and devalue ourselves (think many sports figures, politicians, and celebrities) rather than value ourselves as would be evidenced by stepping up to our problems and finding viable solutions. Denying ownership continually weakens us until we no longer have the strength to even identify the truth, let alone face it.

We've become so accustomed to "fear-based thinking" that it now serves as our native tongue. Do these excuses sound familiar? Which of the following options sound most comfortable to you?

Victim: "I forgot."

100% Responsibility: "Why didn't you write it down?"

Victim: "I didn't have a pen."; "I did write it down but it didn't do me any good because I threw the paper away."; "You can't seriously expect me to remember the details when I've got so much to do."

100% Responsibility: "Simply stated, you didn't care enough about me to keep your promise. And based on your current excuse, I can't count on you to care about me to keep your future promises either. You care more about your petty, immature, self-centered self than others."

Or how's this?

Victim: "It's not really anyone's fault!"

100% Responsibility: "How convenient. Now neither of us is accountable for what happened, AND we don't have any responsibility for resolving the problem, AND we're noble because we are playing nice and letting each other off the hook."

Victim: "Well, it's just one of those things that happens you know…"

100% Responsibility: "No, I don't know how, nor do I want to be in a relationship where things just happen without genuine cause or reasonable consequence."

Our current culture promotes blame, denial, and rationalization as our native tongue. Far more people speak, understand, *and accept* blame, denial, and rationalization than 100% responsibility. We must wake up and face the brutal facts that we have succumbed to accepting "excuse making" over "keeping our promises" as our national language and that *blame, denial,* and *rationalization* have become our native tongue.

People get in their cars late for a meeting, jump on the freeway, and call ahead on their cell phones indicating they will be late, as if this excuses them for leaving late. They left their office late but somehow calling from a cell phone on the freeway excuses that!

We sit through countless meetings where we are bored and unproductive. Rather than confront the truth, we simply slide away in our minds to places unrelated to the meeting's purpose. We don't take responsibility for our role. We are dishonest. Hundreds of thousands of dollars are wasted daily simply because we accept living in our society of victims with our pathetic, victimized state of mind.

Obesity is at an all time high in America—for the old and young alike! Yet we continue to offer our children junk food options right on their school campuses AND drive through fast food restaurants for dinner. We value "saving time" more than "saving lives," which is evidenced by our daily choices involving our youth. If teachers were allowed to teach math or reading as incorrectly as administrators allow children to eat improperly, there would be an outrage among parents. However, despite our knowledge of the facts, we irresponsibly allow this health epidemic to bury our future.

Why are we doing this to ourselves and those we love?! Why do we ignore our responsibilities both at home and in the work place? Two thoughts: Limited Leadership and Undeveloped Emotional Muscle.

Limited Leadership

You can't lift anyone higher in life than you have climbed yourself. We can't expect leaders to teach what they haven't learned and lived. Children at home and employees at work quickly learn how to speak the "native tongue" of their family and work environments. How those in leadership positions respond to life's challenges determines how others respond as well. If we are exposed early to *blame, denial,* and *rationalization* of our thoughts and behavior, we soon mimic what we see and express what best facilitates our success in any organization.

Try and learn a new language once you have become accustomed to your native tongue. Unless you learn early to embrace new ways of thinking and behaving, change later in life becomes extremely difficult to accomplish.

Does your child hear blame or justification as the initial parental response to life's challenges, such as, "The government has done it to us once again," or "Our neighbors are so lucky. Life always seems to go their way," or "I would love to help at my son's school (lose weight, get out of debt...), but a single parent can't be expected to do it all."

Does a new employee hear blame or rationalization as the initial company response to poor market conditions or difficult customer service? "We can't give raises when customers don't pay their bills on time," or "No company can expect to make money in these horrendous market conditions," or "We have tried everyway possible to satisfy our customers but nothing ever works. They are impossible!"

Check your culture—both at home and at work. How effective is your leadership with your children and/or employees? Do you have an inherent flaw in how you express ownership for taking responsibility for your relationships? Are you congruent with your behavior in the work environment and your home?

If your response sounds anything like "Well, I would be if only..." you are not 100% responsible and are undeserving of membership in the club that gives you complete control over yourself and your relationships in life. Your limited leadership will continue to plague you and those with whom you do business.

"The report would have been done but my assistant became ill at the last minute. Sorry." (As if "sorry" dispels any ownership for resolving the problem *or* the other person's dilemma which you've created.)

"I already said I'm sorry. You didn't have to be so mean about it. It's not like I meant to have an affair (crash the plane, lose the deposit). I already feel bad enough without you getting all bent out of shape."

From irresponsible to noble in three seconds. Remarkable! No accountability for creating the problem. No ownership for resolving the problem. However, fully expecting the other party to recognize our misfortune, feel sorry for the mess we're in, and crown us for our noble effort of feeling bad because we're irresponsible, we injured the other party, and/or caused them emotional pain. Yet we can't recognize what we did or why we did it, and we have no intentions to resolve it. Simply amazing.

One reason we accept our victimized mentality comes from being wronged by those we trust to teach us correct principles. Whether we are considering our personal or professional lives, we must recognize the leadership roles we play regarding our children and our subordinates. We have responsibilities that must not be passed along for others to teach. The greatest liability comes when we realize how we neglected to teach others in our care how best to navigate life. If we are irresponsible, we do serious damage to their perception of truth, ownership, and 100% responsibility for their life relationships.

Undeveloped Emotional Muscle

Jorge Cruise, a highly respected physical fitness expert, wrote in his popular book *8 Minutes in the Morning* (HarperCollins, 2003), "Although aerobic exercise is essential for strengthening your heart and lungs, it is not the most effective way to get lean. . . If you focus on aerobics, your body shape will stay the same, even if you burn enough body fat. If you are currently shaped like a pear, you will look like a smaller pear."

If you are in poor shape about taking and teaching 100% responsibility, you must lift weights in order to change. You can not simply run as usual and expect a different result. You may even believe what I am saying makes sense, but remain unwilling to lift weights because you prefer aerobics. You must swallow the "humble pill" in order to begin changing the shape you are in. You must see yourself as having intrinsic value in order to accept your flaws and mistakes. General Lee liked himself and could therefore own his limitations and errors in judgment. Can you accept the consequences of facing your mistakes?

Lifting weights requires a daily regimen and discipline in order to make a difference. Many people in leadership positions are like young children suffering from underdeveloped muscles. They may want to be seen as strong but have not yet consistently lifted enough weights for the proper muscle development. Accepting full responsibility for your life and the relationships in your life requires valid emotional maturity. Becoming emotionally mature requires the same consistent, disciplined approach as becoming physically fit. We must face ourselves honestly if we ever hope to have the mature muscle necessary to be members of the 100% Responsibility Club.

A Life Sentence

One young man who never even applied for membership in the 100% Responsibility Club comes to mind. He was tried, found guilty, and sentenced to life imprisonment for murder. He pleaded for the judge to grant him one last request before going to prison. He simply asked to whisper something to his mother who sat sobbing in the courtroom. Permission granted, the young man with hands and legs in chains leaned down to share what appeared to be a very tender moment.

Suddenly the mother was screaming. Blood flowed everywhere. The young man was apprehended and quickly shuffled away. Order was finally restored and people were aghast to later discover that the guilty young man had tried to bite his mother's ear off.

Days later the young man and his attorney sat alone in his cell. Deeply frustrated that his client could do something so abusive and provocative, he demanded an explanation for why the young man had tried to bite his mother's ear off. With a sullen face, the young man looked at the floor and simply said, "She knew the very first time I stole something and never did anything to stop me."

This young man took no accountability for his actions. He believed that it was his mother's responsibility to teach him to do so. He chose to be a victim who couldn't stop himself from a life of crime unless his mother somehow successfully intervened on his behalf. He felt no ownership for his choices and subsequently had no power to affect positive change in his life.

The victim culture can't work because in it, there is no trust. There can be no trust in relationships based on excuses, blame, denial, or rationalization. We have taken the path *more often traveled by* and that has made the tragic difference in the limited quality of our lives. We duped ourselves into believing we could trust the victim culture to lift and feed us, but sadly now, find ourselves desperate and wanting. Unless we acknowledge that our native tongue is killing our souls and destroying our lives, we can never know the abundant lives we were meant to live.

THE STATE OF "WHAT CAN BE"

Let me create a picture of what membership in the 100% Responsibility Club requires and its subsequent rewards. I'll explain specifically why every family and business, every culture, must embrace it in order to succeed.

Membership Requirements

Membership in the 100% Responsibility Club requires a commitment to getting the desired results as opposed to immediate ego gratification. It requires performance over excuses— empowerment to resolve problems over justification for mistakes.

Simply stated, you must first be willing to be wrong and admit it to others when you are. Second, you must be willing to make right whatever you did wrong.

Membership dues in the 100% Responsibility Club are tough to pay because we've spent a lifetime convincing ourselves that being right was more important than performance and achieving the desired results. Whatever relationship you want, you can have, if you will take 100% responsibility for getting it. You cannot, will not, must not, let any excuses, blame, or justification exist for explaining it away. Being right is far less important than building legitimate relationships—both personally and professionally. A lifetime of being right produces weak people and limited transactions. *A lifetime of taking 100% respon-*

sibility for building legitimate relationships makes strong individuals capable of strong leadership.

Until you can recite the following motto with conviction, you cannot be in the club. Only legitimate club members understand and accept this motto without excuse or exception.

Club Motto

"I am 100% responsible for every relationship in my life I will do whatever is necessary to achieve the desired results. This is not a 50-50% proposition. It is not 100-100%, where both are equally and fully responsible in order for the relationship to work. It is solely and always 100-0%. If there is any blame, it is mine. No excuse is legitimate, sought, or accepted. I am 100% responsible for creating what I get. And I get exactly what I deserve."

Membership Rewards

By taking 100% responsibility for every relationship, we expand our options. We increase our control over ourselves and all factors that have an impact on the relationship. Take anything less than 100% and we limit our options to create high performance and get the desired results. Wouldn't you rather be in charge of your destiny than have someone else control your life?

1. Value yourself enough to be wrong.
2. Respect yourself enough to own the problem.
3. Trust yourself enough to seek proactive resolutions for solving problems and building legitimate relationships.

Being 100% responsible frees you to act…to create solutions…to win! If you give any percentage of responsibility away to other people, they can hold you hostage. If they don't behave as you expect them to, they own you. A long time ago, someone probably lied to you and suggested that the best way to navigate life was to assume as little responsibility as possible. They did you a huge disservice and now is the time for you to hear and embrace the truth. Becoming 100% responsible for yourself and your relationships is the right thing to do. Like a daily regimen of lifting weights, it is challenging, but with proper emotional fitness, it is tremendously freeing.

Join the 100% Responsibility Club. Stop making limited transactions and start building positive relationships for life. Learn to speak a new language—a language that frees and empowers you both personally and professionally. Start lifting weights and developing responsible muscles. You can create an abundant life by refusing to accept the current "victim" culture. Step up and seek 100% Responsibility as a way of life—the way you choose to live! Join this powerful club today. Allow me to challenge you to develop legitimate emotional muscle and become empowered to create successful life relationships.

MAKE LIFE PITCH TO YOU

Whether you like it or not, life always pitches to you on *your* terms. You have the right and the responsibility to carve out your own unique swing while at the plate, and you decide whether you strike out or connect for a base hit. You have the right to expect life to pitch balls in your strike zone.

Good hitters make life pitch to them. They may be able to hit the many pitches in a pitcher's arsenal—fast balls, knuckle balls, curve balls, even spit balls—but they never swing at a pitch that won't get them to first base. They simply don't chase bad pitches.

Don't let life dictate the tone of your game. When you are

PLAYING LIFE TO WIN

up to bat, it's up to you to decide how you're going to react and what you're going to learn from each experience.

· · · · · · · ·

"When I was young, I would listen to my subconscious, and my subconscious would always tell me what the pitcher was trying to do."
– STAN MUSIAL

· · · · · · · ·

All your life you will feel the pressure to be someone other than who you were born to be—to put aside the gift of your unique personality and strive to be someone else. Can't you hear the background chatter as you step up to bat? "Hey batter, hey batter, hey batter—swing!" All your life you will face people who have their own agendas about you—about how you should live your life. Remember, you're in the batter's box, not them!

Kurt Cobain, rock music icon and former lead singer of the Seattle-based rock group Nirvana, forgot this important lesson when he stood in the batter's box. Following his quick ascent to fame as the pioneer of grunge rock music, Kurt committed suicide. In a letter he wrote prior to his death, he explained that he felt guilty for not getting excited about playing his music for his hordes of adoring fans. He said that he felt like a fake and was tired of pretending. His tragic death may have been avoided had he found out who he truly was and remained true to himself. He closed his letter with the statement, "It's better to burn out than fade away"—the sad soliloquy of a gifted man who tragically swung at one too many bad pitches. Kurt judged his life solely by how he thought others saw him, rather than getting comfortable with his own swing. His remarkable talent could have blessed future generations if only he could have found a way to express himself honestly and become the man he wanted to be.

Too many of us place damning limitations on our lives simply because we let idle chatter from behind home plate persuade us to give up our signature swing and go for the bad pitches life so freely offers up to us.

CHAPTER SUMMARY

Points to Remember
- "We must be the change we wish to see in the world." ~ Mahatma Gandhi
- Taking 100% responsibility for your life expands your options for success.
- The best players emphasize personal responsibility over personal rights.

Questions to Consider
- Who role models taking 100% responsibility best in your life?
- What prices are you paying in your relationships for not taking 100% responsibility?
- Who deserves an apology from you?

Application Exercise #1

CERTIFICATE OF MEMBERSHIP

I willingly take ownership of my life. Blaming others, justification, and excuses are unacceptable. I choose to become 100% responsible for expanding my life options and creating successful relationships regardless of inherent frustrations or challenges that may come. I seek membership in the **100% Responsibility Club**.

Name: _____

Signature: _____ Date: _____

Witness: _____
Date: _____

Witness: _____
Date: _____

Chapter 6

Keep Your Eye on the Ball

THE MOST COMMON phrase in all of baseball is "Keep your eye on the ball!" It's so basic, yet so hard to do when a batter steps up to the plate. Why? Because there are so many other distractions that vie for a batter's attention.

Keeping your eye on the ball in life requires paying attention to the way you want to live your life and swinging only at the pitches that will get you there. What do you want your life to be about? What gets in your way and causes you to lose sight of how you want your life to be? You must pay attention to how you deal with life's challenges and figure out what you need to improve about yourself in the process. It requires connecting the dots—looking for patterns in your life that explain why you strike out.

. . . .

"Character cannot be developed in ease and quiet. Only through
experience of trial and suffering can the soul be strengthened,
ambition inspired, and success achieved."
– HELEN KELLER

. . . .

Those who don't pay attention allow the pitcher to dictate
their fate at the plate. Trust me, life will strike you out. I have
worked with so many people who lost ten years of life before
they woke up and realized they had been standing in the batter's box letting perfectly good pitches go by. It is no contest
when you pit yourself against life unless you keep your eye on
the ball.

Opportunities for self-awareness often come unexpectedly.
Of course you must be willing to pay attention when they do.
Life events like marriage, a new job, the birth of a child, and
financial futility all reveal who we are, whether we like it or
not. When life hits you with a wild pitch, consider what it says
about you and reflect on what you can learn about yourself in
the process. How we respond to the pitch speaks volumes
about who we are.

. . . .

**Some of the best opportunities to pay attention come
when you get hit by a pitch.**

. . . .

When I was twenty-five, life stung me with an errant pitch.

I would never have invited this challenging experience on my own so I have life to thank for throwing it my way. I took a group of high school students on a survival course that would make TV's *Survivor* look like *The Price Is Right*. Looking back, I still can't believe I did it, but at the time I was young and thought I was immortal, so naturally my life was all about new adventures. With my naïveté stowed away in my back-pack, a group of teenagers and I set off to test ourselves against the majestic and brutal backdrop of nature.

Roughing it in the wilderness, we carried only the clothes on our backs and relied on each other for warmth to survive the cold nights. We sucked muddy water through the heels of our socks for a few drops of liquid to soothe our parched lips. On the seventh day we killed a sheep with our bare hands in order to ease our hunger. It was admittedly one of the most physically and emotionally exhausting challenges any of us had ever faced in our lives.

Considering the extent of the turmoil we endured, it was interesting to see who was able to "take their hits," and who made a beeline back to the dugout for safety. Ironically, the two most physically fit participants—two male athletes—couldn't emotionally deal with the various challenges and hitch-hiked home, rather than endure the hardships. The one I expected to give up first, a pudgy young 16 year-old girl, stuck it out, and helped us all learn more about who we were through her remarkable endurance. Throughout the trek, this young ill-suited hiker with blisters on her feet would walk along by me and share her perspective on the emotional fortitude she needed to evoke within herself in order to endure the physical pain. The final night each of us slept alone with three matches to build a fire. If our individual fires went out (or never started) we were invited to return to the base camp for more matches or stick it out alone in the darkness.

This young girl, with remarkable endurance and blisters blazing, couldn't start her fire but decided to spend the night alone in the dark. When another participant crossed her path en route to the base camp for more matches, the two decided to stick out the night together without the light or warmth of the fire. That night they forged a friendship so strong that years later, both insisted on having each other as maids of honor at their weddings.

Before the two-week course was over, I knew myself far better than when I began the trek. Some things I liked and some I didn't—but all of it was me. This experience and many others have opened my eyes to me—my hopes, fears, preferences, and dreams. Life throws each of us opportunities to discover ourselves; we simply have to pay attention to what it throws and how we respond if we want to know who we are.

Paying attention allows you to assess how you naturally react to any given challenge and helps you improve because of it.

CHAPTER SUMMARY

Points to Remember
- Know the way you want to live your life, then keep your eye on the ball!
- Look for the patterns in your life that are keeping you from getting onto first base.
- If you don't pay attention to the pitches, life will strike you out!

Questions to Consider
- Have there been opportunities for self-awareness that you have not noticed, and so have not taken advantage of? At what cost?
- How do you respond when life throws you a wild pitch?

Application Exercise #1
Think of a recent interaction you've experienced and consider these three reflections that help you keep your eye on the ball:

1. Why did you react in the way that you did? (What about you caused you to react that way?)
2. Were you being true to yourself in the way you handled the situation?
3. What about your behavior could you have changed or improved?

Chapter 7

Be a Hitter

ONE OF THE most fascinating aspects of business consulting for me has been how the best leadership teams are always more willing to address why they're losing, while weaker teams want to talk only about their wins. Strong leaders welcome dialogue about where they need to improve individually and as a company, while insecure leaders generally skew feedback to reveal only the positive half-truths about themselves. Leaders willing to see how they swing at life enjoy a much higher batting average than those too insecure to look.

. . . .

"It was a great honor to win a batting title in those days.
It wasn't an easy thing to do."
– GOOSE GOSLIN

. . . .

The mark of genius is wanting to see all of what you are as well as what you could become.

How accurately you see both your strengths and limitations

will determine your batting average. In baseball, a player's batting average is the ratio of hits to at-bats, or in other words, how reliably a player will land on base when up to bat.

In life, one's batting average is best represented by his or her emotional intelligence or EQ. First identified in the early 20th century as social intelligence, among other names, emotional intelligence gained significant notoriety in 1995 with Daniel Goleman's best-selling book by the same name. Emotional intelligence is comprised of five distinct life skills (the foundation of which is self-awareness) that enable an individual to navigate through life far more effectively than those without them. The five skills are self-awareness, self-regulation, motivation, empathy, and social skills.

Recent studies have shown that EQ is dramatically more important than IQ when it comes to achieving success in personal and professional life—four times more important, according to a recent Harvard study. And yet, among a child's basic education of reading, writing, and arithmetic, self-awareness is blatantly ignored. This is perhaps because we have such a shortage of people competent to teach it.

Individuals who are accurately aware of themselves enjoy genuine self-esteem because they accept their limitations as well as their strengths. They even hunger for constructive criticism and are willing to risk looking foolish when making necessary changes.

To be a hitter, you must be fully aware of and value who you are and how you naturally respond to the challenges of life. To deny your true core is like refusing to accept that 2+2=4. What is the point?! If you can't accept simple addition, you can never enjoy complicated mathematics. Such is life. *If you can't get yourself, you can't possibly hope to get others.* If you can't see yourself honestly and value who you are, you will never get on first base, let alone cross home plate and score.

CHAPTER SUMMARY

Points to Remember

- If you want to increase your batting average, pay attention to why you're losing.
- To score in life, you have to value who you innately are, and be aware of how you naturally respond to the pitches life throws at you.

Questions to Consider

- Can the people in your life trust you to get a hit when you get up to bat?
- Do you seek constructive feedback from those in your dugout?

Application Exercise #1

Go to www.hartmancommunications.com to order your Character Profile Packet. You will receive 6 Character Profiles. Complete one profile on yourself, then ask five people representing various aspects of your life to fill one out on you as well. Compare the results and make a commitment to focus on developing antidotes to your three most disabling personality flaws.

First Base: Section Summary

*No other base in the game of life is solely
about you, so take advantage of it.*

This is the only base on which you are invited to be completely yourself—to see yourself in color—to discover your
own signature swing and use it at the plate. This is the one time
in the entire game of life you get to do exactly what you want
to do, and what you do best. Just remember, you're up to bat to
move players around the bases.

You must be a hitter. To get a hit means you must develop
an accurate self-awareness. You must discover and value your
signature swing by figuring out who you innately are, as
defined by your driving core motive. Your signature swing
asserts you have a legitimate weapon—something you can trust
to get you on base and move your teammates around the bases.

First, embrace your style. Come to know and like yourself
for simply being you. Learn to blend your innate and developed gifts in order to win at the game of life.

Second, you have to create a winning support team in your
dugout. Select people who want you to win—who want to win
themselves. Use your teammates to get you around the bases.

Third, you have to step up to the plate—pay attention and
get on base. If you don't swing at the pitches life throws your
way, you've wasted an "at bat" and lost a chance to get on first
base. Take 100% responsibility for getting a hit and getting on
base when you're up to bat.

Once you master all three principles, you will step up to the plate with confidence. You won't have to accept the bad pitches life throws your way or simply hope life treats you kindly. You can be highly proactive in sending a very clear message to life that you are fully engaged in the game and confident that you will leave your mark. You can challenge life to throw you pitches you know you can hit.

Questions to Consider

- What will you do with your life? (When it's over, what will you be remembered for in your life?)
- How can you make life pitch to you so that you don't waste your time swinging at wild pitches?
- Can you remember a time life hit you with a pitch? What did you learn?

Rounding First Base

Once you're on first base, anyone can throw you out. It's no longer simply a duel between you and the pitcher. You are now a target for everyone in the field. No ball players want the inning to end while they are standing on first base. You must now focus on reaching second base. While getting to first base was a rather daunting challenge in itself, it is only the first step in playing life to win. You must keep the game's larger picture in perspective. Players who spend too much time celebrating getting on first, often miss opportunities for getting to second base and eventually scoring.

You can't get to second base while keeping one foot on first. Getting to second base requires accepting that there are certain truths in life, and it's up to you to embrace them or fight against them. While some are absolute and some are personal, how you deal with them determines your success in the game.

Arnold Schwarzenegger learned the power of truth when he first arrived on American soil as an immigrant and moved to Southern California. Almost at once, he ascertained that money was the seat of power in his new home, and instead of fighting it (which would have been natural for someone recently removed from a strong socialist environment to do), he accepted it. Knowing himself and his ultimate desires, he maximized his strengths and minimized his limitations against the light of truth in his new environment (the power of money) to build a very rewarding life. His Hollywood career aside, he positioned himself to be a strong advocate for positive change—from his national fitness advocacy programs as the Chairman to President George H. W. Bush's Council on Physical Fitness and Sports to his successful bid for the governorship in California in 2003.

First base is only ninety feet away from second base. What are you going to do? Are you leading off first at every pitch, looking for your opportunity to sprint to your next goal, or are you safely, yet timidly, stationed on first, too afraid that you'll get thrown out? You must let go of your insecurities, because once you get to second, you are in scoring position. Getting to first was all about you, but from here on out, you need to forget yourself.

Next base: seeing the truths about you and your life. Life makes much more sense when you are correctly aligned with the rules of the game. Remember, the fact that you don't want to face the truth does not change the truth. *The sooner you get aligned with truth, the less energy you'll waste ignoring, denying, or rationalizing away your limited life.* Getting to second base enables you to honor the best of who you became by arriving on first base. Recognizing the truths of life further enhances the best in you.

SECOND **2** BASE

Get Truth

FACE THE BRUTAL TRUTHS OF YOUR LIFE.

· · · · · · · ·

ALL LIFE IS ABOUT RELATIONSHIPS.

· · · · · · · ·

YOU GET WHAT YOU DESERVE.

Chapter 8

Step 1: Face the Truth

"Rather than love, than money, than fame, give me truth. I sat at a table where were rich food and wine in abundance, and obsequious attendance, but sincerity and truth were not; and I went away hungry from the inhospitable board."

- HENRY DAVID THOREAU

SECOND BASE IS now ninety feet away. The distance between bases remains the same regardless of who's at bat. The number of strikes and balls each batter gets doesn't change regardless of where you are in the batting line-up. And *American Idol's* Simon Cowell isn't wrong on his assessment of the hit T.V. show's young upstart singers, no matter how rude he may seem. Second base is all about substance over style. It's not about how you appear or how you look, it's about who you really are.

Some things in life are simply absolute. A runner who is tagged out only one inch shy of reaching second base may feel cheated. He may blame the distance between bases, claiming that the bases are too far apart. But all of his ranting doesn't change the fact he didn't go the distance. So it is with us. We cry foul when life has treated us unfairly, or a life lesson has been particularly painful. Rather than facing the truth, we often run from it.

Some people refuse to believe that there are absolute truths in life. My dad was one of them. For him, all truth was relative and should be interpreted against the circumstances of one's environment. Those who hold onto this comforting, albeit inaccurate notion miss out on the liberating power that confronting truth affords.

In his well-researched book *Good to Great* (Collins, 2001), Jim Collins reveals the five most critical elements that separate great companies from simply good ones. Standing out as a dominant theme in his research is the power of truth. According to Collins, "great companies make...good decisions—a direct result of a person's willingness to confront the brutal facts."

What are the brutal facts in your life that you refuse to face? Most notably we hold on to bad employees longer than we should, stay in limited relationships to "have someone" when we know it's not a fit, eat poorly more often than not...well, you get the idea. Sticking your head in the sand will not absolve you of the consequences that denying the truth will inevitably shower upon you. Accepting candid feedback from those with whom you interact may be initially painful, but ultimately freeing. Stop thinking that you are somehow special and therefore exempt from life's absolute truths! You can no more wish life to be different than the runner on first base can wish second base to move closer. It will never happen in this lifetime so give it up and accept that certain truths remain intact for every legitimate relationship.

I was recently working with an executive team in Southern California who excels in their emotional intelligence. Over the past five years, most of the team members have worked hard to see themselves accurately and improve themselves, which in turn has enhanced the entire team. Their leader is an intelligent, business savvy, people-oriented individual who has always offered his players the opportunity to win both personally and professionally—he constantly encourages them to grow up and pay their dues by facing the truth about themselves and changing accordingly. This astute leader assures that his staff's abundant technical skills and strong IQ are balanced with their emotional intelligence.

From day one of my intervention, the Chief Financial Officer has struggled with the relevance of doing his EQ work. He made the decision to remain "limited" and stay behind while the team moved to the next level. He refused to develop his emotional intelligence and see the truth about himself and how he holds the team together. Undoubtedly, his resentment for not getting the leader's job earlier in his career remains one of his strongest impediments to facing the truth about himself and enjoying the successes of his colleagues. This team member's predicament illustrates the tragic nature of ignoring the truth—if you don't face it, you'll face the consequences.

As this executive team discussed the various people who had fallen off the team over the past five years, it became very apparent that they all shared one thing in common: none of them ever faced the truth about themselves. They never "got it"—no matter how many times they had the opportunity to do so. Not one of them could see what everyone else saw around them. They simply refused to see it.

I let a young man go from my company and told him to call me when he finally realized what he was giving up by refusing to improve himself. He was a very capable individual who came from a scarcity mentality (best to selfishly take care of myself first). He remained blind to how others saw him. His talent created praise, which fed his insecurity in such a way that he listened only to the positive and dismissed all negative feedback as irrelevant. Sadly, he has already begun building a wall over which he will not be able to climb without humbling himself (which time and experience may do for him) and allowing the truth about himself to get on his radar.

THE TRUTH ABOUT LIES

The hard part about facing the truth is that it's not always pretty—aspiring to a glamorized version of it is so much more attractive! Fabrications seem so much easier. They often start out with good intentions, and before we know it, we've fooled ourselves into believing them. It's almost a natural tendency because lies usually glorify the truth more than they contradict it.

In the 2003 movie *Big Fish,* the character Edward Bloom spends his entire life spinning tall-tales to make himself into something bigger than he is. Born out of the desire to leave an enhanced (albeit inaccurate) legacy with his wife and son, he creates a fantastic image of his life that eventually envelopes him. When his son, William, sets out to sort out the fact from the fiction, he discovers that his father's incessant tall-tales were merely attempts to ensure that his memory lasted longer than he did. "That was my father's last joke, I guess," William admits, "A man tells his stories so many times that he becomes the stories. They live on after him." But behind the fabricated façade, who was he really? And why wasn't he enough simply being himself?

In the words of American psychologist and philosopher William James, "There is nothing so absurd that it cannot be believed as truth if repeated often enough." Fiction may be easier to accept than truth is, but it's how well you can align yourself with the truth that determines whether you can get to second base! William Bloom's search included going back to the people and places that were in his father's fabrications, looking for clues that would help him separate the truth from the falsehood. In our own pursuit of truth, bad liars are easy to spot—the heavy blinking, the increased perspiration, the avoidance of direct eye contact. Similarly, there are certain signals that reveal if we are unable to face the truth about ourselves. Inconsistent behavior is one of them. A White who may be acting like an angry Red at work, but a kind White at home, may be refusing to face some professional truths about himself.

I recently ran into a former client of mine who had declared bankruptcy, but was afraid to tell me about it. While we were talking, I asked him, "How's business?" And the best he could do was to say that he's in a partnership he can get out of, should he choose to. Nice job of softening the truth! While his response may have indeed been true, the reality was that his business had failed. How sad that this man felt so insecure that he had to spin falsehoods so that he could deem himself acceptable to me.

It's no secret that living a lie can actually seem more comfortable than facing the truth about ourselves; and frankly, society provides little consequence for being someone you're not. In fact, our world teaches that we should become someone we're not by rising from our roots and achieving international acclaim and recognition. Oddly enough, arguably the highest paid people in America are paid to lie. Film and TV actors make millions portraying lies on camera and are consequently adored for it. The only problem is, while everyone enjoys the momentary bliss of their fabrications, they fail to realize the long-term effects of avoiding the truth.

I was recently sitting with two leaders of a highly successful company discussing a key employee and his status with the company. In our talks, one of the men chose to withhold the truth about his plans for promoting this key employee. (He was probably thinking that if it didn't come up, he wouldn't have to lie about his intentions!) Following our discussion, this executive promoted the employee in question without informing the other leader. While the promotion was ultimately denied when the senior leader learned of it, perhaps the greatest tragedy of this situation was the complete loss of trust that resulted between these two company executives, a loss of trust that eventually destroyed their professional relationship. It's always interesting to me how often people legitimize the withholding of truth as though it's any different from flat out lying. It isn't!

The very second your twisted thinking convinces you to withhold truth, please know that you are creating a lie that will cost you time, self-respect, and often money to correct. Dishonesty is one of life's most demanding mistresses. What feels good at the moment will prove costly in time.

I could write volumes about getting to second base. It is the position I played in Little League as a boy. It is the role I play most often in my career. Other bases typically carry a more glamorous allure. Second base, for me, has its own unique magic that is unclouded by pomp and circumstance. It's solid and consistent. Second base serves as the anchor in baseball— it lines up with home plate and creates a structure that promises each base lies ninety feet apart. Getting to second base requires that you accept absolute truths, which you can always set your watch by.

As an American, second base is my Midwest—always holding the country together with its simple, timeless sense of right and wrong. Midwesterners' strong integrity and legitimate values play a vital role in keeping this great nation in check. They refuse to jump too quickly for new fads created in the West, and are less inclined than their East Coast neighbors to take themselves too seriously. They face life and its many hardships with an optimism that says, "Truth has been a good neighbor. We've both shared each other's space long enough to trust each other to go to bed at night without locking the doors or turning on the lights. We know we'll both be right back at each other with the same expectations the next morning."

CHAPTER SUMMARY

Points to Remember
• Facing the brutal truths about your life liberates and empowers you.
• How honestly you align with truth determines whether or not you'll get to second base.
• Omission of truth is no better than commission of lies. They are both forms of lying.

Questions to Consider
• Who gives you honest feedback about how you live your life?
• How do you typically react when life treats you unfairly?
• Who are you currently withholding truth from? Why?

Application Exercise #1
List three times in your life when you have been completely honest with yourself and others. What was the outcome of your brutal honesty?

1) _____
Outcome: _____
_____
_____

2) _____
Outcome: _____
_____
_____

3) _____
Outcome: _____
_____
_____

Chapter 9

Key 1: Be Humble

"I hate advice unless I'm giving it."

– JACK NICHOLAS

TO GET ON first base, you have to get yourself; to land safely on second base, you must face yourself. Your self-awareness is a critical component for seeing the truth and accepting its absolute nature in your life. Lessons learned en route to first base apply here. After discovering your signature swing, you learned how to value what you discovered, limitations notwithstanding. Your ability to face yourself requires seeing your strengths and limitations in light of how they impact your life and the lives of those around you. Ironically, the more you value yourself, the more comfortably you face yourself against the backdrop of absolute truth.

Humility is the cornerstone of facing yourself and confronting the truth. In the timeless classic *The Neverending Story,* the boy Sebastian was given a set of seemingly insurmountable tasks, the last of which required him to face himself in a mirror that revealed who he truly was. "Greater men have run from the mirror only to return a shell of who they once were," he was warned. It is not the courage of men, but rather the vulnerability of a child that ultimately enabled Sebastian (and us!) to successfully get past the mirror. In fact, rather than running from the mirror, as so many others had done, Sebastian welcomed what he saw and walked right through it.

Humility welcomes questions and resists always having the answers. It is objective and non-judgmental. Humility says that while we may be "good enough and smart enough," as *Saturday Night Live's* Stuart Smalley would always say, we still have room for improvement.

Unlike the "good enough, smart enough" affirmation, we can't rest on the laurels of one good deed or one positive change. We should relish our successes and be anxiously engaged in creating more successes. Stringing many successes together creates an abundant life.

Humility provides you with the courage to see the truth for what it is and eliminates the biases that your own strengths and limitations, preferences, and blind spots inevitably create. Without humility, you will always misjudge the distance to second base, increasing the likelihood that life will throw you out!

CHAPTER SUMMARY

Points to Remember

- Humility is valuing your strengths enough to honestly embrace your limitations.

- Childlike candor frees us to see ourselves without disguise or retribution.
- Pride is never satisfied with merely having or being. Pride requires that you have and be more than another.

Questions to Consider
- When was the last time that you laughed at yourself in public?
- With whom are you most likely to act superior and/or least humble? Why?
- Are your blind spots more likely to be physical, intellectual, emotional, spiritual, social, or financial?

Application Exercise #1
If you want to face truth, you have to face yourself first—you have to look in the mirror. When you do, what do you see? Does your reflection scare you or is it surprisingly delightful? What negative traits stand out? What excites you about you? What do you need to change? It can be a horrifying experience, but if you take responsibility for what you see, your reflection will improve every time you look. Record your thoughts here:

Chapter 10

_____

_____

_____

_____

_____

_____

Key 2: Eliminate Insecurity

INSECURITY IS HUMILITY'S greatest enemy. Ours can be a cruel world. Sadly, we witness disparity, corruption, and selfishness every day. Fear typically lives at the root of these illnesses. I believe that all people want to live happy and successful lives. Unfortunately, insecure people don't trust that they can be happy and successful if others are too! Rather than humbly approaching their lives, accepting what is right and facing what is wrong, they lie to themselves and hurt others with their lies. In their fear, they often wreak havoc in the lives of everyone with whom they cross paths, including their own. Yet, despite mounting evidence against them, they actually believe they are the legitimate ones who see most accurately how things should be done, how life should be lived, and how the bases should be run.

With the passage of time, however, their faulty thinking begins to unravel and such insecure individuals become obsessed with creating new faulty truth filters in order to hide how truly limited their own lives have become. In the end, they are unable to find satisfaction or sustain happiness, and inevitably blame others—anyone and everyone, including life itself—for their demise. They are often heard making absurd assumptions such as "Someone moved second base!" or accusations like, "You can't trust anyone anymore!" In truth, from the very beginning they refused to take any ownership for the chaos they created, the cruelty they imposed, and the false truths they worshipped.

In John Powell's revealing book *Why Am I Afraid to Tell You Who I Am?*, he explores the uncharted territory of phony facades, born from our fear of facing the truth, and delves into the pitfalls and traps we set for ourselves as we create our own faulty truth filters. Since reading his book many years ago in college, I have often wondered why we allow ourselves such limited passage in a world we were meant to experience so abundantly. Thirty years as a therapist and corporate interventionist have led me to conclude that beneath it all, we don't trust that we are good enough. We fear rejection, inadequacy, and simply not measuring up. So we lie to ourselves because we are afraid to face the truth—afraid to see ourselves honestly, without façade or protective filters—filters we eventually come to accept as reality, filters we sadly come to believe are genuinely us.

This whole notion of creating façades and protective filters is woven throughout our entire culture. For example, the fashion industry has recently been exposed for changing sizes on clothes to reflect Americans' increasing girth. Rather than force customers to admit they've gained weight, designers have simply increased the measurements of each size, so people feel better thinking they are fitting into the same size when they're not. Talk about "feel good" lies. However, it doesn't change the truth.

Fear and insecurity debilitate us by creating falsehoods we

inevitably accept as truth. Our hands may tremble in fear of facing ourselves naked and vulnerable but over time we discover great strength in the power of humility. It's the only thing that can align us with truth.

Ironically, our insecurity drives us from the one thing we should trust the most—who we are. And that's the magic of second base. It carries no glamorous allure; it simply is. The constancy of truth is what sets second base apart as an important step in the game of life. Just as the North Star remains constant in the universe despite earth's rotation, second base remains our North Star of truth. By its very placement, second base becomes a remedy for insecurity—a safe and constant reminder of where we stand in the great game of life.

CHAPTER SUMMARY

Points to Remember
- Facing truth is a critical step toward becoming secure with yourself.
- Insecure people survive daily life by shielding themselves with faulty truth filters.
- You are good enough simply being you. Believe that and your life will come together.

Questions to Consider
- In which aspect of your life are you most insecure: physical, emotional, intellectual, spiritual, social, financial? Why?
- In which aspect of your life are you most secure? Why?
- Where did you first learn to lie to yourself? How were you rewarded for it?

Application Exercise #1

Place a sign on your mirror that says "I am lovable and therefore capable of loving others." Repeat it out loud to yourself daily.

Application Exercise #2

Read Scott Peck's *The Road Less Traveled*.

Application Exercise #3

Stand outside at night and look at the North Star. Ponder who and what have been your North Stars in your life. Write a thank you letter if appropriate, or write your thoughts in a journal.

Chapter 11

Key 3: Take 100% Responsibility

IF YOU WANT to get to second base, refuse to blame anyone for anything in your life. Take 100% responsibility for every relationship you encounter and you will find a tremendous surge of personal power that will lift you over obstacles, which will end the inning for others.

We live in a victim society where accepting responsibility and blame for our shortcomings has become increasingly uncommon. We have learned that we can always let ourselves off the hook by offering excuses or blaming others who don't do their part. While it may be easier to shift the blame for our limited lives, the long-term effects are disastrous. Those who consistently blame others for what happens in life ultimately have no life. Eventually, when very little is "your responsibility" you have very little life! Just consider organizations you belong to where you have little responsibility. How engaged are you? How concerned are you compared to places you have major responsibilities? When you have relegated yourself to innocent bystander or fringe patrol in your new life, you're in serious trouble.

Being 100% responsible frees you to act, to create solutions, to win! Membership in the 100% Responsibility Club requires a commitment to getting the desired results regardless of the consequence. It requires performance rather than making excuses—empowerment to resolve problems over justification for mistakes.

. . . .

"Personality can open doors, but only character can keep them open."
– Elmer G. Letterman

. . . .

In order to be 100% responsible, you have to be willing to be wrong, and you have to be willing to do what it takes to make things right. It's a call to action—that's the power behind 100% responsibility. Membership dues in the 100% Responsibility Club are tough to pay, because we've spent a lifetime convincing ourselves that being right was more important than performance and achieving the desired results. Whatever legitimate relationship you want, you can have, if you will take 100% Responsibility for getting it. You cannot, will not, must not, let any excuses, blame, or justification exist for explaining your life away. Being right is far less important than building legitimate relationships—both personally and professionally. A lifetime of being right produces a weak person and limited transactions. A lifetime of taking 100% responsibility builds strong individuals capable of creating legitimate relationships.

CHAPTER SUMMARY

Points to Remember

- Charactered people refuse to blame anyone for anything in their lives.
- You can have any legitimate relationship you want, if you are willing to take 100% responsibility for it.
- When your relationships are more important than being right, you'll feel richer and happier inside.

Questions to Consider

- Are you willing to be wrong in your most intimate relationships?
- Are you willing to make things right, whatever it takes, in those same relationships?
- Who role models 100% responsibility best for you in your personal life?
- Who role models 100% responsibility best for you in your professional life?

Application Exercise #1

Remember taking your Hartman Character Profile for Chapter 7. Go back to the final page of your profile and assess the three limitations you deemed most dysfunctional in your life. Now complete the following exercise by refocusing on the three areas of improvement you want to make a reality in your life.

List three of your limitations and the color they correspond to. For each limitation, list one strength that will remedy that limitation and its corresponding color.

LIMITATION	COLOR	REMEDY STRENGTH	COLOR
1.			
2.			
3.			

If I were a stockbroker on the New York Stock Exchange of life, I would always advise clients to invest in second base. It's always a strong buy because it's always undervalued while it over performs. People rarely give it the credit it deserves, but that doesn't change the strong return on investment you'll consistently receive by investing in it.

Chapter 12

Step 3: Absolute Truths

GETTING TO SECOND BASE puts you in scoring position. Facing truth creates tremendous hope and momentum in your life. Refusing to face it literally wears you out and renders you a captive to first base! How can something so simple, so basic, remain so elusive in our lives? What is it about truth that makes this base such a challenge? Why is doing the right thing so difficult?

. . . .

**Runners can score on a base hit from second base.
Facing truth puts you in scoring position.**

. . . .

Ralph Waldo Emerson once said, "Everything has its price." Facing truth can be painful—usually is at the time. But ignorance exacts an even greater price—one you often pay more than once before it's done with you. Truth, perhaps the most underrated principle in life, remains an old friend who never lies to us and whose advice always makes us feel better when we take it.

Last year I was seated outdoors at a restaurant next to a woman effortlessly smoking a cigarette. I watched, mesmerized as she enjoyed one of the biggest health hazards known to man, asking myself how anyone could smoke with all the information we have regarding the devastating impact cigarettes have on human life. Meanwhile, I was drinking a diet soda filled with enough caffeine to make me stay awake for the next forty-eight hours. I drank a lot of sodas. With poor diet and physical inactivity poised to become the leading preventable cause of death in America, here I was doing my part to become just one more statistic.

Obesity is killing America. A new study shows that obesity-related health-care costs reached an estimated $75 billion in 2003, and taxpayers foot the bill for about half of those expenses through government sponsored healthcare programs like Medicare and Medicaid. My poor food selection and lack of exercise went against every physical fitness tip known to man, and while I was judging this woman and her choice to smoke, there was little difference between her and me—I had simply picked a different substance.

I still don't know why *that* day impacted me with such fervor. It has been over a year since I faced the truth about myself and confronted my poor fitness habits, and while I still have a ways to go, I take solace in the fact that I am moving toward a worthy goal. For so long I simply refused to face truth and make improvements in my life. At least with physical fitness, I am finally on my way to second base.

Truth has a way of revealing itself through time. In my counseling, I have always found it very easy to answer a client who questions whether to leave a relationship or not. My answer is always the same—it is your right to decide to stay or go, but you will know the wisdom of your decision (or lack there of) in six months. In that time, you will either become a better, stronger rendition of yourself or you will be in a bigger mess than you are right now.

Truth always emerges, whether we like it or not. It is always there and always will be. The decision is ours whether or not to accept it. We can welcome it now, face the brutal truths we are ignoring, and reap the benefits, or we can wait until it's too late. Eventually, our faulty truth filters will be revealed for the fabrications they are in the limited lives we accept.

Success breeds success. Once you successfully confront any absolute truth and align your life with its principles, you feel more energized and confident to face truth in other critical areas of your life. Any step that brings you closer to second base empowers you to see, trust, and embrace all absolute truth.

Absolute truth is like math. It doesn't matter how good you are at it or how much you resist it. The numbers always play out the same. For example, there's no denying that $2 + 2 = 4$. No one in their right mind would propose that $2 + 2 = 7$. The same goes for absolute truth. Life, like math, is bound by inalienable truths, whether we "get" them or not. You may struggle with getting life's equations as much as I did with math. Personally, I was never much good at it. However, your struggles don't change the equations you need to learn in order to successfully navigate life anymore than my resistance to math changed the numbers. You do the math. History is replete with examples of natural consequences that follow peoples' willingness to face (or reject) truth. From King George's failure to accept the American Colonies' growing dissatisfaction to Marie Antoinette's naïve inattention to an impoverished people, failing to face the facts has dire consequences.

CHAPTER SUMMARY

Points to Remember

- 2 + 2 = 4. As it is with math, so goes it with truth. You cannot force false numbers to add up!
- Facing truth creates tremendous hope and momentum in your life.

Questions to Consider

- Emerson said, "Everything has its price." What prices are you currently paying that are too high?
- What physical health truths are you ignoring today?

Application Exercise #1

Write down three absolute truths you believe in and live by in your daily life. How has your life been enriched by doing so?

1) _____

Benefit:_____

_____

2) _____

Benefit:_____

_____

3) _____

Benefit:_____

_____

★ ★ ★ ★ ★

Absolute truths are not something we are taught very effectively in our current culture. We are often left to our own devices to stumble across them, which can be painful and difficult to fully grasp. Just as I want you to understand motives, I want you to know the powerful relevance that absolute truths play in your life. They are pivotal in creating abundant, legitimate lives. To get started, I want to introduce you to three absolute truths that you must embrace in order to safely land on second base.

Chapter 13

Absolute Truth #1: All Life Is About Relationships

"Our lives are shaped by those who love us, and by those who refuse to love us."

– JOHN POWELL

FOR ALL OF MAN'S modern conveniences, we have yet to discover a technological advance that simplifies relationships. Isn't it ironic that with the internet, cell phones, and other advances in communication, finding a good relationship seems more difficult than it used to? With every opportunity to increase interpersonal relationships we continue to struggle to make sense of something as simple as everyday dialogue with each other. More fish in the ocean perhaps? Not likely. We just don't get it. Making life about relationships requires a major paradigm shift—from things to people—a commitment to work on ourselves and value others.

At the heart of every relationship is communication. No matter how you spin it, your ability to effectively communicate dictates the quality of your relationships. Becoming a more effective communicator requires paying attention to your limitations in order to improve the process of interacting with others. We would never accept dial-up internet when a high speed connection is available, yet we willingly accept bland communications that beset our relationships. Why can't we learn to value human connections and pay the dues necessary to create legitimate relationships that are at least in the same ballpark as our technological advances? At the end of the day, how we engage each other is far more important than how far we have advanced in our technical applications.

One of the biggest stumbling blocks to better interpersonal communications is that they're exactly what their name suggests: personal. Developing relationships requires a personal commitment to trust and a willingness to reveal the truth about our-

Three EQ Traits You Need to Improve Your Relationships

1. Social Skills:
• An ability to find common ground and build rapport

2. Self-Regulation:
• The ability to control or redirect disruptive impulses and moods
• The propensity to suspend judgment to think before acting
• Discipline yourself—create a system for success

3. Motivation:
• A passion to work for reasons that go beyond money or status
• A propensity to pursue goals with energy and persistence

(Adapted from *Emotional Intelligence* by Daniel Goleman, Bantam 1997)

selves. It requires facing each other heart to heart, which can be uncomfortably invasive and intimidating. Today we are far less vulnerable sending emails to one another because we maintain a comfort zone that encases our intimate and innate selves.

· · · · · · · ·

Perhaps nothing is more difficult than realizing that we have feet of clay–that we are not all we hoped to be.

· · · · · · · ·

Truth is truth however, and regardless of our insecurity, the most meaningful connections in life come between people who have learned how to love each other. The art of creating legitimate relationships should be required curriculum in our classrooms, and should be considered as critical as other "life skills" we promote such as reading, writing, and arithmetic. Relationship skills should be rewarded with the same public approval, as well.

Creating quality, enduring relationships is one of our most noble aspirations in life. We must pay attention to the absolute truths that make this noble aspiration a reality for us. We must not abdicate this responsibility. We must raise the standard if we expect our youth to embrace the notion that quality lives include nurturing, quality relationships. When I see international intrigue with celebrities' or political leaders' broken marriages, spurned relationships, and selfish intentions, I become deeply concerned. Let celebrities act in movies, gifted athletes play sports, even politicians govern—but don't give them sway over how you live your life.

The weakest link always controls the relationship. It's sad, but it's true. No relationship can be any stronger than its weakest member. Becoming trustworthy, learning to accept others' imperfections, and caring about others enough to develop listening and verbal skills are a few critical ways we can ensure that we don't find ourselves on the losing end of life's version of the recent television game show. "You are the weakest link. Good-bye."

THE PERSONAL AND PROFESSIONAL DIVIDE

I have always found it intriguing how some people are so much better at professional relationships than their personal connections, while others fail miserably in the professional arena despite their strong personal relationships. While most people are usually strong in one of the two areas, very few are strong in both.

I can think of many professional men and women who exude remarkable strength in business only to become limited victims in their personal lives. They refuse to be anything less than extraordinary in one arena while accepting unfulfilling roles in another.

Beth comes to mind. Passionate and articulate, she faced her career with the utmost confidence. Nothing frightened her. She challenged her colleagues legitimately. She was always a strong player on every business team, and highly sought after. She left it all at work! Single, frightened of men, Beth would quickly capitulate to their demands in order to keep them interested and yet her track record demonstrated no one lasted more than two dates. She withheld her beliefs if she sensed they might prove controversial. Everything she was at work she wasn't at home. Beth had no confidence in herself or her ability to sustain legitimate personal relationships. It took two years to create a belief system in herself that she could trust and use to build upon in her personal life—two long years to equalize her legitimacy at work and at home.

. . . .

How we navigate long-term relationships tells more about us than any other single aspect in our life.

. . . .

The irony of the personal-professional divide is that it doesn't actually exist. It's nothing more than a figment of our imaginations—a barrier born of our own insecurity. How you act in one life arena should be congruent with the other, though that is rarely the case. Remember, first base was about getting yourself and keeping congruent with who you innately are, and you are not being congruent if you present different versions of yourself in different contexts. The defining factor appears to be a sense of self-confidence (or lack thereof), which determines how effective each of us becomes in either area of our life. You learn by doing. The sooner and better you engage others, the more natural the process becomes.

Nothing will ever replace the importance of legitimate relationships—whether they are positive or negative. Becoming sure of oneself in both personal and professional arenas frees us to accept and relate to others more comfortably.

CHAPTER SUMMARY

Points to Remember
- All life is about relationships.
- The weakest link always controls the relationship.

- How we engage each other personally is far more important than our technical expertise.

Questions to Consider

- Are you stronger in your personal or professional relationships?
- Who sets the standard for you in what a legitimate enduring relationship looks like?
- What specific relationship skills are you currently developing?

Application Exercise #1

Ask yourself the following four questions. The first two questions query who has been significant in your life. The last two questions query in whose life you play a significant role.

1) Who has loved you most effectively in your life?

2) Who has blocked or least understood you most in your life?

3) Who do you currently love most effectively in your life?

4) Who are you currently blocking or misunderstanding most in your life?

Chapter 14

Absolute Truth #2: We Are NOT Born Equal

ONE ACTION THAT *will always get you thrown out en route to second base is comparing yourself to others.* We all come in different packages; it's a fact. Diversity truly is the spice of life. Why can't we accept that? Only humans find it necessary to compare themselves with others. While making comparisons might prove helpful if your motivation for doing so is healthy (i.e. a role model for what you could learn to do better or in appreciation for what someone else brings to the relationship), such a practice usually proves debilitating, as the comparison typically comes at someone's expense, including your own.

The mistaken assumption that we are all born equal creates incorrect standards and a false sense of security for anyone who buys into this *faulty truth filter.* An individual with a debilitating handicap, for example, may look at another who does not share his handicap and say, "What is wrong with me? If we're born equal, why am I this way?" and all the while he will ignore his own value and consequently his own opportunity for growth and development. Similarly, a superior athlete may look at a fellow teammate with inferior athletic prowess and claim, "I am better than my teammate, and thus have no need to learn from him." In both situations, the comparison creates a limited and incapacitating perception that impedes the necessary individual growth required to cross home plate and score in life.

It's always been interesting to me that we usually regard differences as limiting, such that we even try and hide them. Truth is, the more we value our differences, the stronger we become, and the quicker we get to second base. The individual who values his handicap may find strength in other areas that exceed that of the person he compares himself to (for example, blind people often enjoy a higher capacity to use their other four senses), while the superior athlete who values the inferior teammate may learn the power of becoming a team.

The only true equality in the human race is our innate value. Though different in every imaginable way, we are equal in value. One human being, regardless of his stature or position, should be esteemed equal with his fellow human beings. Accepting that we are not born equal legitimizes our self-esteem, in spite of our differences.

SELF-ESTEEM vs. SELF-CONFIDENCE

It's really a shame that self-esteem and self-confidence are frequently identified as interchangeable synonyms in our society today. We are often led to believe that if you have one, you have the other. Not so. Self-esteem and self-confidence are two completely different traits, though each has its place and value.

I learned what true self-esteem is from a woman I never actually met, her story relayed to me by a patient from Northern California. "We would always go skinny dipping in the river," she said. "A group of us would pack a picnic and spend the day together. What fun we had! My best girlfriend was rotund and honestly looked like a beached whale all sprawled out on the riverbank. Her boyfriend was gorgeous. He looked like a model because he was so good looking.

"And this woman—my whale of a friend—she never worried about him wanting to be with other women or other women trying to pick him up. She was never concerned with her boyfriend getting second looks from other women. Absolutely NO jealously! NO fear! Just this marvelous beached whale propped up on a pillow and laughing up a storm, swapping jokes and inviting delightful conversation. She absolutely loved people and she definitely adored herself. For the life of me, I don't understand why. To look at her, you certainly wouldn't think she had any reason to feel so good about herself!

My patient's last sentence struck me like a bolt of lightening. She adored herself and had absolutely no apparent reason to do so! "That's it!" I said, "That's true self-esteem!"

Looking back now I can honestly say I felt like I had discovered gold. What a rich insight into one of the greatest maladies of our day. She didn't value herself because of anything she produced, how she looked, or anyone of status that she knew. She liked herself simply because she breathed.

When you think about it, there are no prerequisites to join the human race. Self-esteem is your standing invitation to accept yourself because you breathe. You have been given this awesome opportunity to live, and the mere fact that you are participating in this wonderful experience called life attests to your tremendous self-worth. Self-esteem is not just words, or even actions, for that matter. It is an attitude of simply being. If you do nothing more than accept that you have been chosen for the team of humanity and appreciate the magic you bring, then you have true self-esteem.

* * * * * * *

Self-esteem comes simply because you breathe; while self-confidence comes because you proactively do.

* * * * * * *

Self-confidence, on the other hand, is something completely different, and doesn't even come from the same roots as self-esteem. Self-confidence is a result of your successes, your abilities, and the mark you leave daily on life.

To illustrate the difference between self-esteem and self-confidence, think of the two as separate and unique mountains. If you wanted to build self-esteem, you would have to climb a completely different mountain than you would for self-confidence, and vice versa. In fact, once you've climbed one mountain, you have to completely descend it before you can begin climbing the other. Self-esteem and self-confidence are no more similar than the different treks to the top of each mountain. Climbing one mountain does not mean you've automatically climbed the other.

I can still see this famous, world-class artist sitting in my private office, telling me how he, at the very young age of ten years, decided to be the best at what he did professionally in order to compensate for his feelings of inadequacy. He said that he wanted desperately not to be a "nerd" or an outcast from his friends. However, all his early attempts at social connection left him feeling inadequate and more determined than ever to over achieve in order to fill the void he felt when comparing himself socially with his classmates.

He succeeded in earning tremendous adulation from the world, but remained completely baffled at why his success had never filled his ever-expanding void and need for self-acceptance. He simply believed that once he had climbed the mountain of self-confidence, he could take a flying leap across the divide to the mountain of self-esteem, and that his success would fill his personal void. He failed to realize that the hikes to achieve self-esteem and self-confidence are not the same, and require completely different skills and tools.

Some children are born with a substantial sense of self-esteem. They like themselves from the beginning and resist any attempts by unhealthy parents or others to change that perspective. On the other extreme, some come out of the womb struggling to accept that anything is right about them. While acceptance of their innate strengths is difficult, they eagerly embrace their innate limitations. Tragically, many who are unable to see or accept their innate strengths, often abandon them in search of others' gifts, which they deem more valuable than their own.

It's unfortunate that so many in our society mistake strong self-confidence for high self-esteem. In the thirty years I have worked intimately with people, it has become powerfully clear that self-confidence medallions such as athletic prowess, good looks, or celebrity status have nothing to do with people internally liking or accepting themselves. In fact, our county courts are full of records of individuals, who should have enjoyed a great life, but died prematurely by their own design because they didn't like or accept themselves. On the other hand, I have worked with people from diverse genders, races, religions, and socio-economic origins who, by all standards of success in this society, should have simply tossed in the towel at birth, but who chose to create and enjoy remarkably rewarding lives instead.

Building your self-confidence will never create legitimate self-esteem. Self-confidence comes from productively "doing," while self-esteem comes from simply "being."

Nature accepts herself, why don't we? Animals, plants, and other living organisms accept their roles in life, while we struggle to see the legitimate value and purpose in our existence. It's painfully clear to me that people with low self-esteem resist their natural beauty, to a fault. They are uncomfortable in their own skin and constantly struggle to change who they are on the outside because they feel certain that once they become someone else, they will be at peace with themselves. Sadly, people like the renowned artist I spoke of can spend an entire lifetime looking elsewhere for the magic of self-acceptance when the mountain of self-esteem they must climb begins in their own backyard.

Before you can climb the mountain of self-esteem, you have to know where on the mountain you currently stand. While everyone is at a different point in their mountainous ascent, the chart below illustrates a general distribution of where the four motive-driven personality types naturally fit on the spectrum of self-confidence and self-esteem.

Notice that those with a high self-esteem find little need to control others, while those with a low self-esteem are more likely to push the control valve.

	High self-esteem/ Low need to control others	Low self-esteem/ High need to control others
High self-confidence Low self-confidence	Yellows Whites	Reds Blues

Unfortunately, lack of self-esteem has become an overused and abused excuse for not stepping up to the plate and taking 100% responsibility for life. Those with a high self-esteem may deem character building and personality development activities a waste of time simply because they are already content with themselves, while those with low self-esteem may use it as a crutch and feel incapable of rising to the challenge of change.

CHAPTER SUMMARY

Points to Remember
- We are NOT born equal, yet remain equal in value.
- Always check your motive when you compare yourself to others.
- Self-confidence comes from doing, while self-esteem comes from being.

Questions to Consider
- What has been your greatest handicap in life? How have you dealt with it?
- Who is the best example of self-esteem in your life?
- Are you more critical or forgiving of yourself in life? Why?

Application Exercise #1
List two activities you will commit to becoming more skilled at in order to improve your self-confidence.

1) _____

2) _____

Chapter 15

Absolute Truth #3: You Get What You Deserve (and You Continue to Get What You Allow)

IN HIS THIRD LAW of motion, Newton proposed that in every interaction between two entities, each exerts an equal and opposite force on the other. "For every action, there is an equal and opposite reaction." For example, when you sit on a chair, you are exerting a force on the chair that is equal and opposite to the force that the chair is exerting upon you, thus enabling you to sit on the chair. The third absolute truth is much like Newton's third law. For everything you do, there is a corresponding reaction, and quite often that reaction isn't what you expected or intended.

One of my childhood friends has always proclaimed to know more about every business than any boss for whom he has ever worked, to a fault. Truth was, he was overwhelmingly arrogant and considered himself a cut above everybody else, including his boss. Over the past thirty years he has never held the same job for more than one year and has been on welfare assistance repeatedly—all because he was so bent on looking better than everyone else that he was unwilling to face the brutal facts of his life and what might be wrong about him. My friend wrongly assumed that he could change the distance between life's bases to suit himself.

Unfortunately, his wife was no different. She lived in collusion with him rather than challenging this twisted thinking. In marrying each other, they got exactly what they deserved. In fact, I recently discovered a letter written to me by his wife over thirty years ago in which she laboriously complained about how misunderstood her husband was by his employer at the time.

Our response to life's events determines what we deserve.

"You get what you deserve" means you are 100% responsible for the actions—and reactions—in your life. Some people like to call it karma; I call it truth. Your life is more about what you do and how you react than it is about what happens to you.

· · · · · · · ·

Remember: What you are doing is what you would rather be doing!

· · · · · · · ·

Take life's various crises for example. Most people face between three and seven totally devastating experiences in their lifetimes—experiences that are emotionally, spiritually, physically, or psychologically life threatening. In such traumatic events, we place most of our focus on the experience itself, rather than on how we respond.

Embracing this vitally important truth (that you get what you deserve) requires taking an in-depth look at what you are doing from another's perspective. You've heard of "thinking outside the box," this is thinking outside yourself. What do others think of your communication style? How do you impact your personal and professional relationships? Why do you deserve them?

Ironically, people are prone to neither see nor accept their roles in both the positive and negative relationships in their lives. For example, many single women constantly critique and challenge the legitimacy and value of single men, yet wonder why they can't create a positive connection with one, without ever seeing the role they play in their own demise. Ironically, while they are busy criticizing, other single woman are discovering and creating rewarding relationships. We must be willing to see the role we play in every relationship in order to understand how we are deserving of it, whether it be positive or negative.

This applies to professional relationships just as much as it does personal ones. I am often fascinated with companies who do not truly value the customer. They cut corners at the customer's expense. They refuse to consider the customer's needs when creating new products. They even blame the customer when sales drop rather than looking at themselves. Yet, they claim they put the customer first in their business. It is never easy looking at ourselves and seeing the truth—especially when it's negative.

What's more, the truth can even be hard to accept when it's positive. I have known many people who refuse to see their great value, continually self-deprecating when they are actually quite talented, legitimate, or capable. And for all their genuine gifts, their lives remain limited because they see themselves as such. As tragic as it is, individuals who refuse to see their innate worth deserve the limited life they receive.

Look at your life and connect the dots. What works in your life and what doesn't? What role are you playing in your personal and professional relationships? You make all the difference. After all, it's something about you that invites the type of relationships you have with others. Once you see what that is, you can begin to improve your role in your relationships. Until then, you will remain the victim of others' choices and your own twisted thinking.

YOU CAN NOT *NOT* LEAVE A LEGACY

Perhaps the boldest argument for embracing this absolute truth that *"you get exactly what you deserve and continue to deserve what you allow,"* comes in seeing the final lasting mark you leave in life. When you die, how will people remember you? No matter what your decisions are in life, everything you do leaves a mark. In the end, your life—and getting to second base—adds up to exactly what you put into it. When I yell at my computer because it misbehaves, my technology gifted cohorts always smile and say "garbage in, garbage out!" The same is true for the abundant life filled with legitimate relationships—magic in, magic out! My father always gave his grandchildren a crisp $1 bill for each year they were old on their birthday. The money was nice, but the effort he took to go to the bank, prepare early so he would always have crisp dollar bills to hand out for every child's birthday created a legacy that I have continued in his honor ever since after he died.

You determine the numbers that will eventually add up to what your life becomes. Trying to change the math never changes the truth, or final outcomes. *Every generation brings unique challenges creating opportunity to leave unique legacies. Some things remain constant, while others change. Relationships have been and will forever be with us. Learn to build legitimate relationships; most of what you do in life will be forgotten. Very little is remembered. How you make people feel will always last longer than you do. Create a connection that makes people feel legitimate and loved for having been in your life.*

CHAPTER SUMMARY

Points to Remember
- You get what you deserve, and continue to deserve what you allow.
- You live in collusion when both parties deny truth in favor of accepting faulty truth filters.
- What you are doing is what you would rather be doing.
- You can not NOT leave a legacy.

Questions to Consider
- If you could choose to do anything, live anywhere, and be anyone, what/where/who would it be?
- Why are you choosing the current life you live?
- Who would you like to invite into your life?
- Who would you like to invite to leave?

Application Exercise #1
What you are doing is what you would rather be doing. If you disagree, then prove me wrong. Nothing would make you happier than to live your life congruent with what you say you

value. List three life activities you promise to make part of your life this year and do what you say you would rather be doing.

1. _____

2. _____

3. _____

Make it happen or accept that what you are currently doing is what you would rather be doing. The choice is completely yours to make.

Rounding Second Base

YOU ARE NINETY feet away from third base. Your entire focus has sifted from self to truth. The game intensifies with each base you tag. You are now in scoring position and must keep your head in the game. Perhaps the most intriguing part now is how the game shifts completely from you to others. Third base is all about getting over yourself so you can enhance the lives of others.

How many times in life have we seen people who think the world revolves around them? How often have we seen business and personal relationships destroyed because one or both parties were consumed by selfishness? You will never score in life as long as you think you are more important than others. However, we can't get others until we get over ourselves—our insecurities, our petty issues, our selfishness.

The pitcher (life) has his back turned toward you. He is busy working on the player in the batter's box. You are completely on your own now. You can lead off. You can score on a hit. You can make a difference if you can get over yourself.

First base (getting yourself) was all about personality—your innate strengths, limitations, needs, wants, motivations, and preferences. It was fun being all about you and made getting into the game both inviting and exciting. But it really was ALL about you—what you bring to bat, how you swing at life, and how you get on first base.

Third base (getting over yourself) is all about character—

strengths developed throughout the game that were not innately yours at home plate. Getting over yourself is all about preparing yourself to make life about others. Getting to third base brings the unique challenge of winning the game of life by scoring as a team rather than simply on your own.

. . . .

"You give 100 percent in the first half of the game, and if that isn't enough, in the second half you give what's left."
— YOGI BERRA

. . . .

Rounding second base brings unique challenges of its own. Suddenly the base path seems tighter and being thrown out becomes more likely. *The three most critical elements required for each base runner to "get over self" and tag third are (1) selflessness, (2) focus, and (3) balance.* It is no longer about simply playing to your strengths as popular psychology suggests. This base demands that you give up your limitations and focus on a legitimately balanced life.

. . . .

Perhaps nothing goes more against human nature than having to face our innately flawed selves.

. . . .

Get Over Yourself

**YOU ARE THE REASON THAT
LIFE DOES/DOESN'T WORK.**

· · · · · · · ·

**GETTING CAUGHT IN LIFE'S PICKLES
GETS YOU THROWN OUT.**

· · · · · · · ·

LIVE YOUR LIFE SUCH THAT OTHERS SCORE.

Chapter 16

Moving from Selfish to Selfless

CONSIDER WHAT HAPPENS when a young couple decides to have a child. Everyone says that it completely changes your life, but no one knows what that really means until they do it. Having a child completely changes how you spend your time and money—how you prioritize your entire life. Even the day preceding the birth, your entire life is yours to live without regard for the care giving of another human being. Yet, the minute the child emerges from the mother's womb, that all changes!

The birth of a child helps parents *get over themselves*. While they "once upon a time" could stay out late, party, and sleep late in the mornings, they are suddenly thrust into taking the baby into consideration before making any plans for themselves. Some parents adjust better than others. It all depends on their emotional maturity. Some get angry and actually blame their distress on the newly born child whom THEY created! They refuse to give up their freedom, making life choices with only their perceived best interests in mind.

The following journal entry comes from Kathleen—a frustrated Yellow mom who felt overwhelmed caring for others while losing herself in the process. She entitled it "I want to be twelve again!"

TUESDAY, JANUARY 25

All I want is to be 12 again. Twelve, thirteen, even fourteen would be way better than my miserable life today! Relatively no problems—no babies constantly calling, crying, clutching, pawing. And if I needed someone to talk to, I could just call a friend. I want my old best friends back who sided with me whether I was right or wrong—just because we're best friends. I miss being on the same wave length—don't have to explain 'cause they already understand.

I want to cry and rage and blame everyone else again! I want to have my worst problem be what to wear to the school dance, or will he notice me, or how can I get my parents to lend me some money.

I remember 12 as a great time—washing dishes was the most tiresome thing imaginable. I basically did what I liked, except on week nights. I want to be 12 because the weight I worried about was much less than the 25 extra pounds I face today.

I want to be 12 because it wasn't always MY house that needed cleaning, or MY responsibility that daily chores are done—making beds, laundry, watering plants, dusting furniture, mopping floors, and doing dishes (I still hate them!).

And it doesn't stop there. If I take a break, there is that much more I have to catch up on. I want to be 12 because I didn't have two babies to feed and endless diapers to change. I didn't have a husband who demands breakfast, lunch, and dinner AND my sympathetic ear to come home to after my maddening day with kids!

I want to be 12 again because I didn't have to be responsible.

It has never been my long suit. I prefer FRIVOLITY once again!

Others are willing to get over themselves in order to enhance the quality of their child's life, ultimately discovering that life becomes more legitimate when sacrificed for others. It feels more rewarding than merely living for yourself.

In the book *Tuesdays with Morrie,* Morrie was asked by Mitch Albom about having children. Morrie suggested that having a child was the only time when a person would feel the complete and utter reliance of another human being on them for survival. In order to succeed, the parent must abandon some of his or her own needs (*selfishness*) in order to facilitate the child's development (*selflessness*). Something always has to give and it must come from the parent who *hopefully* has the capability of giving it.

So why do so many give up living life on their terms in order to give birth to a child? What is so wonderful about children that causes an adult to share their time, money, and life itself, in order to give this stranger a place in their hearts and space in this world?!

Like the game of baseball, getting to third base requires someone else doing something (like hitting the ball) in order to help you score. So it goes with the game of life, in which we need others to help us see ourselves honestly and get over ourselves in order to live legitimate lives. Kathleen was frustrated. We all get there from time to time when we stretch to reach third base. She didn't yet realize what a gift she was giving herself in learning to make her life more than simply an easy, limited, and self-serving journey.

And children merely represent having someone in your life with whom you are willing to share space, time, attention, yourself, and your life. Children, and all others who need you to become selfless in order to facilitate their lives, can motivate you to get over yourself and make life about someone or something other than you. Some people never learn this lesson and find themselves frustrated, yet confused as to why they aren't getting around all the bases. They don't understand that they are making it impossible for themselves to score.

* * * * * * *

"Make the most of yourself, for that is all there is of you."
– RALPH WALDO EMERSON

* * * * * * *

Thus the game becomes about relationships—giving and getting, inviting others' strengths to compensate for our limitations, etc. We actually need children and others in our lives to enable us to reach third base. Often the element of our lives we resent most is the very thing we need to help us score.

* * * * * * *

"The task is not to aspire to some heaven but to make everyday life divine."
– DR. GOVINDAPPA VENKATASWAMY ("DR. V")

* * * * * * *

The paradox of getting safely to third base requires playing to our strengths (*personality*) while simultaneously addressing our limitations (*character*). This is a juggling act on the high wire of life. You must know what you do well and what needs repair. This requires an interesting blend of humility and self-confidence. One with out the other assures that you will be tagged out.

The first essential element for getting over yourself is moving from selfishness to selflessness. *The idea that life is best lived while serving others flies in the face of selfishness.* In order to live life abundantly, you must learn how to get over yourself. Becoming selfless requires trusting that you will be all right without always having your needs met. Still you must set legitimate boundaries so that others do not needlessly take advantage of you. Selflessness demands accepting delayed gratification rather than having the childish notion that you must have whatever you want whenever you want it. It is a constant struggle to make your life about others rather than demanding that it continually be about yourself.

I recently asked a group of distinguished professionals to think of one individual in their lives whom they would describe as *"a great human being—someone they saw as a mentor to them."* Then I asked them to use only one word to describe this individual. The following descriptions are their memories of these remarkable individuals who clearly learned to get over themselves, and subsequently left a profound legacy.

Solid, charisma, balanced, unshakable faith, selfless, caring, teacher, loving, kind, forgiving, sacrificing, humble, simple, happy, connected, perspective.

Do those words reflect how you are seen by others? I asked the same group of people to think of an individual who epitomized the opposite of greatness and describe them with one word. The following descriptions were shared:

Selfish, takes credit, lies, insecure, fear-based, irrelevant, uses others, poor self-awareness, insincere, arrogant, doesn't value others, lacks empathy, reactionary to life.

What words or individual lives define greatness for you? Is it Nobel Prize winner Madame Curie who discovered the element radium and the uses of radioactivity? Perhaps you prefer Alexander the Great for his relentless quest to explore the unknown. Is it someone in your family? Is it you? Consider all the people you have personally known. At the end of this chapter you will provided an opportunity to list the three greatest individuals in your life.

· · · · · · ·

**"You cannot hope to build a better world
without improving the individual."
– MARIE CURIE**

· · · · · · ·

I was with a CEO of a company recently whose father took all the credit for the company's stellar success. This White business leader was remarkably insightful and proactive in his leadership. He asked me quietly after one rather intense training session, "Taylor, I have always risen to leadership positions without seeking them out. Still, after all these years, it puzzles me why I am rarely given legitimate credit for the things I do while others demand *and* get the praise. Why is that? And what, if anything, should I do about it?"

I looked him straight in the eye, and said, "John, your greatness lies in your clarity about what needs to be done without the emotional neediness to be recognized for it. While it may be difficult sometimes to see your needy Blue father demand and receive adulation because of his immaturity, it would cheapen you and what you want your life to be about, to demand your well-deserved praise. You would be stepping back rather than moving forward in your quest for personal development and heightened emotional intelligence."

I loved John's honesty about being slighted (*very human!*) and his ability to see that attempting to make others acknowledge his leadership would actually diminish his greatness. It was his ability to serve without demanding praise that made him so much more legitimate than his talented, albeit emotionally immature, father.

The weakest link always controls the relationship! The weakest link in this relationship (and thus the person with the control) was John's father, whose actions obviously affected John very deeply.

Getting stronger, bringing more to relationships requires learning how to make life about others rather than yourself. As you mature, you no longer need to have everything your way. You are comfortable enough with yourself, secure with who you are, able to allow others to have their needs met without feeling cheated yourself. Weak people can't do this. They can't help themselves. Their neediness surfaces often like an ugly mask they can't see but everyone around them can't miss.

The reason most players get tagged out between second and third base is selfishness. *Selfishness is the number one reason relationships fail in life—both personally and professionally.* Selfishness is often disguised such that we rationalize our inappropriate attitudes and/or behaviors until we suddenly find ourselves caught in a pickle.

CHAPTER SUMMARY

Points to Remember
- "You cannot hope to build a better world without improving the individual." ~ Marie Curie

- The weakest link controls the relationship.
- Life is best lived while serving others.

Questions to Consider

- Who is the weaker partner in your most intimate relationship? Why?
- Who are you currently inspiring by how you live?
- How are you currently being selfish with others? How will you change?

Application Exercise #1

List the three greatest individuals in your life. Put one word by each name that best defines why you consider them great.

NAME	WORD DEFINING GREATNESS
1. _____	_____
2. _____	_____
3. _____	_____

Do any of the words strike a chord with you about yourself? In order to achieve greatness in life, we must learn to get over ourselves—our petty, insecure dark sides. We need role-models and life coaches to help us discover our inner greatness. Look for people you can invite into your life to help you become your best self.

Chapter 17

Life's Pickles

THE PICKLE (or hot box) in baseball can best be described as "being caught between a rock and a hard place." The runner finds himself in no man's land, between the bases, trapped between two players of the opposing team who have the ball. The ball can be thrown faster than he can run. (Thus, the dilemma—the pickle—of which base to bet on in trying to land safely.) Typically, neither base looks particularly attractive, but to remain indecisive ensures being tagged out as the opposing players continue to close the gap between them.

Here's the deal. There are only two ways to get out of a pickle safely. The first option is to return to second base without being tagged, which essentially demands that the runner face the truth about himself and his dilemma which created the pickle in the first place. The second option is to make it safely to third base. Getting to third requires that the base runner "get over himself" and become unselfish. It's not easy since selfishness is exactly what got him in the pickle in the first place. In other words, *getting out of a pickle is a most challenging experience because the very reason you got in one in the first place, is exactly what you must get over about yourself in order to get out.* Tough thing to do regardless of which base you decide to approach!

Life's pickles come for a variety of reasons and display themselves in a variety of ways. What they have in common is their selfish nature and complicated ways! Sometimes we find ourselves in a pickle because of twisted thinking. (We overestimate our ability to beat the ball to third base!) *Twisted thinking is always fear based* and most often displayed in forms of ignorance or arrogance. Both can be deadly in life because they are unrealistic and typically land us in over our heads, requiring energy and time to correct—energy and time that could have been more wisely used elsewhere in our lives.

Arrogance comes from insecurity. Arrogant people are always trying to compensate (often unconsciously) for their flaws by acting as though they are something they are not. Sure, arrogant people are irritating to others, but struggling internally with your own arrogance is no picnic either. Arrogant people are so busy compensating for themselves that they often miss out on enjoying real lives and real relationships.

Ignorance comes from a base runner's unwillingness to learn—to pay his or her dues and do his or her homework. People who refuse to see life accurately become limited in their ability to run life's bases. *Ignorance, however, doesn't free us from the consequences.* I remember one couple who refused to buy a home, letting several years go by before committing to their first purchase. By the time they were ready, the real estate market had eclipsed their buying power and they remained frustrated renters while raising their family. Getting to third base requires alert eyes and minds and ignorant people often find themselves missing key opportunities to score. The most deadly ignorance comes when a base runner *doesn't know what they don't know.* Prices must still be paid.

Let's take an individual who is married and chooses to have

an affair. Having the affair places him (or her) in a "pickle," which he justifies for any number of reasons—none of which will change the fact that he can't land safely on third base until he quits the affair. All the excuses in the world don't change the fact that he is being untrue to himself, to his partner, and to the person with whom he is having the affair. Yet thousands of people choose to have affairs. Why? Because they would rather meet an immediate need than face the truth about themselves and their marriages. They would rather find solace in another's arms than do their homework, get over themselves, and legitimately fix their lives.

Affairs don't solve the problem. Never have and never will. Still everyone who engages in an affair somehow thinks they are unique and exempt from "being caught in a pickle and tagged out." The only hope for the person in an affair is to either go back to second base, which requires getting the truth and honestly facing themselves, or moving to third base, which demands that they get over themselves. Either way they must give up the affair.

Getting to third base requires a higher standard of play than getting to first or second does. It means valuing yourself enough to let go of making life all about you and learning how to make it about others.

I see people stumble between second and third all the time. They remain stuck between the bases and blame anyone or anything (but themselves!) for why their base running has stalled. They are emotionally immature and generally seek other emotionally immature people to validate them. Sad to watch (especially if you're a teammate) because you know they are going to get thrown out just when life could have become really interesting!

Don't mistake getting to third base for going home. Getting to third base is about getting over yourself and going home is about getting others. While getting over yourself lays the critical underpinnings for going home, they are very different experiences and require completely different skills. For example, consider the person who always interrupts others while they are talking. He or she talks over the person trying to present his or her thoughts. Getting to third base requires that the person stop interrupting and talking over the other person. Going home requires that the person actually listen to what the other person has to say.

Getting over yourself means not having to make the conversation all about you (having your say). Getting others means intently hearing and listening without judgment to what the other person is trying to say (often unsaid between the verbal lines). Obviously one can not hear well when he or she is trying to make his or her own point heard. *In order to get others, you must genuinely get over yourself.*

CHAPTER SUMMARY

Points to Remember
- Life's pickles are created when one refuses to either get truth or get over him/herself.
- Twisted thinking is always fear-based. It is rooted in insecurity and selfishness.
- The most deadly form of ignorance comes when a person doesn't know what they don't know because they still have to pay the price.

Questions to Consider
- Are you willing to play life at the higher standard required by third base versus first base?

• What current choices are you making that prevent you from getting over yourself?

• Who do you think role-models a life free of making it about themselves at the expense of others?

Application Exercise #1

Tagging third base requires that you give up selfish attitudes and behaviors. List the most destructive self-serving attitude and behavior that you currently have that prevents you from getting over yourself.

Destructive Self-serving Attitude	Destructive Self-serving Behavior

Chapter 18

Time to Grow Up

BEING ALL ABOUT *yourself simply means you never grew up!* Young children require lots of attention. They need others' help simply to survive. Some children grow into adulthood never learning how to make life about others. They continually *require being looked after and being taken care of*—having their needs met!

While children bring tremendous joy, they are difficult. They require constant supervision and attention at the expense of our freedom. Consider how draining it is to be with a forty-year-old who still acts like he or she is in the terrible twos. Sadly, we have all been there with someone...sometime!

Emotionally immature people drain everyone with whom they interact. They become highly manipulative and demanding. *It's all about them and your job is to keep the spotlight on them at your expense.* Tragically, I have worked with many of these adults and they live in absolute fear that they will be exposed and have to "carry their own" or "fend for themselves." This fear drives them to become highly creative in the methods they use to keep others hooked into meeting their daily demands.

If you are involved intimately with someone who is unable to tag third base, your life game has become a tedious bore. And if you're the one who can't get to third base, you're boring. You were born to change, to evolve, to become more than you were at birth. If you keep demanding that others change and meet your needs while you refuse to do your own work, you will find yourself lonely and suffer huge disappointment in life when you finally have to look in the mirror.

THE BLONDE JOKE
A redhead walks into a sports bar around 9:58 p.m. and sits down next to a blonde woman who is having a few drinks.

The TV is on, and the 10 o'clock news is about to begin.

The news crew is covering a story of a man who is on the ledge of a large building preparing to jump.

The redhead turns to the blonde and says, "You know, I bet he'll jump."

The blonde replies, "Well, I bet he won't!"

The redhead says, "I got $20 that says he will."

"You're on!" says the blonde.

Just as the blonde places her money on the bar, the guy does a swan dive off the building, falling to his death.

The blonde, very upset, hands the redhead her $20 and says, "All is fair, here is your money."

The redhead replies, "Honey, I can't take your money. I saw this earlier on the 5 o'clock news and knew he would jump.

The blonde replies, "So did I, but I never thought he would do it twice!"

The blonde just couldn't believe he would repeat the same mistake. We should be equally disappointed in ourselves when we repeat poor choices and create negative life patterns. In order to get over our limited selves and develop our best selves, we must commit to a program of making life about others rather than about only us. The steps in the following chapters will help you successfully *develop your emotional muscle, get over yourself, and get safely to third base.*

CHAPTER SUMMARY

Points to Remember
- Being all about yourself means you never grew up.
- Emotionally immature people drain everyone with whom they interact.
- You were born to change, to evolve, to become more than you were at birth.

Questions to Consider
- What is your chronological age? How old are you emotionally? What is the difference?
- Are you committed to a lifetime of change or do you prefer remaining stuck in a rut?
- What role do you play in making the same mistakes repeatedly in your relationships?

Application Exercise #1
Look back over your life and consider the relationships you have experienced. Consider the relationships that you have experienced similar problems with. What part do you play in creating trouble in your relationships? You create problems by:

1) _____

2) _____

3) _____

FOUR STEPS TO LIFE BALANCE
AND POSITIVE FOCUS

Chapter 19

Step 1: Bring Your Gifts of Life to the Game

Balance who you are with what you want to become.

THE EASIEST WAY to get over yourself is to understand yourself for who you are at your very core. John's ability to be true to his White self played a critical role in his ability to remain ego-free. His immature Blue father created false intimacy with people, desperately trying to pacify his emotional neediness—like trying to fill a glass with a hole in the bottom.

If you understand how you are and why you are like that, you can sort out what about yourself you want to keep and what you want to discard. We live in such educated times, yet *so few of us honestly know ourselves. We are often clueless about what works for and against us in life and this creates serious obstacles that prevent us from getting around the bases.*

The Color Code Personality Profile is a powerful guide to who you were innately born to be. It gives you significant clarity about your inner driving core motivations. This is your unique personal foundation. Begin with this awareness and move to align how you engage life on a daily basis with who you are at your personality core.

Quiet reflection, journaling, group conversations with others who interact with you, family discovery, and self-assessments all can provide valuable insight about what you value and enlighten you about specific patterns you have chosen to use in getting through life. Some are positive and some may be limiting. You want to be very clear about what enhances and/or detracts from your foundation. We often fool ourselves, believing that our limitations and negative behaviors are, in fact, enhancing and we seek to fiercely defend them.

We've all seen elderly people who never made sense of their lives. They never connected the dots and saw how their bad habits got in their way. They never understood the role they played in limiting their own lives.

At the height of the great ancient Greek empire, Socrates suggested that the Greeks' superficial lifestyle was totally missing the point of life. He said, "The unexamined life is not worth living." With today's civilized world of great abundance and technical wizardry, yet superficial pursuit of trivial pleasures, I often wonder if Socrates wouldn't make the same statement to us. His work may have inspired the unknown author who spoke so candidly about the paradox of today.

The paradox of our time in history is that we have taller buildings,
but shorter tempers, wider freeways, but narrower viewpoints.
We spend more, but have less.
We buy more, but enjoy less.
We have bigger homes and smaller families,
more conveniences but less time.
We have more medicine, but less wellness.

We talk too much, love too seldom, and hate too often.
We've learned how to make a living but not a life.
We have added years to life but not life to years.

These are the times of fast foods and slow digestion,
big men and small character, steep profits and shallow relationships.
It is a time when there is much in the showroom window
and nothing in the stockroom.

These are YOUR times—YOUR history—YOUR time to live! Connect the dots between the successes and failures you have experienced in your life and take responsibility for whatever role you have played in creating them. What has your life been about? Where have you spent your time and money and emotional energy—and why?! Have the results been positive, fulfilling—met your expectations?

. . . .

See yourself for who you were meant to become. See others for how you were meant to touch their lives.

. . . .

Angelina Jolie became a superstar celebrity sensation only to discover over time that she preferred the picture her dots created when she was helping disadvantaged people as opposed to pursuing her acting career. She felt more alive with a sense of purpose, using her voice in a different forum than her sole acting focus allowed. She began spending more time and energy on her new focus and felt more honestly aligned with who she was and what she valued.

By connecting the dots of your life, you will quickly see whether past choices, relationships, and/or business decisions have been limiting or rewarding. The results must always align congruently with your personality and value foundation in order for the connecting of the dots to create a positive picture. *When your life choices and relationships lack alignment with who you are and what you value, your life presents itself in chaos and disappointment.*

Don't pass the buck on the work you have come here to do! Face your destiny with the same style as Angelina Jolie. Winners always want the ball when the game is on the line. This is YOUR time and your game is on the line. Greatness comes when we embrace the lives we have the opportunity to live.

CHAPTER SUMMARY

Points to Remember

- You must first "get yourself" in order to "get over yourself."
- "The unexamined life is not worth living." ~ Socrates
- This is YOUR time to live! Connect the dots of your life and map out what your life has been about.

Questions to Consider

- How are your bad habits and/or personality limitations preventing you from living life more successfully?
- What are you refusing to look at that currently wastes time and energy in your life?
- What specific opportunities do you create for examining the quality of your life?

Application Exercise #1

List three activities you currently choose to do and replace them with a value-added activity that would enhance the quality of your life and provide for more rewarding relationships. Commit yourself to the replacement activity for at least one month in order to allow yourself to enjoy the change in focus and perspective. New habits take time in order to take hold. Be sincere and diligent in the change in order to enhance your success.

CURRENT ACTIVITY	VALUE-ADDED REPLACEMENT ACTIVITY
1. _____	1. _____
2. _____	2. _____
3. _____	3. _____
4. _____	4. _____

. . . .

**Focus on doing the right things in order
to get over your limited self.**

Chapter 20

. . . .

Step 2: Face the Truth About Yourself and Your Life Choices

SECOND BASE GIFTS of facing the truths about yourself and what you believe about life are pivotal to getting over yourself. There are many reasons people accept their unrewarding lives. Pride, fear, lack of courage, limited vision, and ignorance represent just a sampling of notable culprits.

This is where you take a hard look at what about you is messing up your program. You must be willing to change direction if what you are doing is working against who you were meant to become. *Change is complicated, but without a true perspective on what you want to become, change becomes impossible.*

Replace a negative with a positive. Move toward a healthy attitude or behavior rather than simply stopping the negative one. You must believe that there is a better way to live your life or you will remain unwilling to do what is necessary to change. Try this equation for change.

D + V + P > C = CHANGE

(*Dissatisfaction* with your life + the *Vision* of what you want to become + positive *Practical solutions* for change must be *greater than* > the *Cost* of living life as you currently are in order to successfully change.)

Combine your dissatisfaction (D) with an aspect of your life and a clear vision (V) for how your life could improve. Connect these with proven practical solutions (P) which you can readily apply to your life and believe that they are greater than the current cost (C) you are paying for accepting your current dysfunction and you will change. Without all these elements in place, change will be an arduous, if not impossible task.

I have worked with young people who left the path set by their parents and/or peer group because they saw a better way to live. Some had mentors like teachers or grandparents; others read books; still others felt drawn by internal maps that led them to change their lives and free themselves from the imprints left by parents and/or peers.

What about you? What personality limitations have you corrected? What life values have you embraced in your efforts to create a meaningful life? What truths do you trust to be constant and legitimate enough to invite change in your life?

Anyone who has faced their limitations knows the difficulty. A prominent minister shared with me how his temper cost him dearly in his youth. His father was his Little League baseball coach. He tagged a runner out at home plate but the umpire called the runner safe and the game was tied. He became so enraged that he hurled the baseball into center field while screaming at the umpire.

"As the ball left my hand, I suddenly realized the inning was-n't over and two more base runners scored because of my loss of control. We lost the game because of me and I haven't for-given myself to this day! My dad was furious with me and I still can't believe what I did!"

Life is about change. It's not about beating ourselves up for mistakes we make. However, we must pay attention to what we do right and what we need to work on. Life can get away from us if we don't face ourselves and make the necessary adjust-ments to bring out the best we can be.

While my wife and I raised our family, we were fortunate to have two key babysitters who helped with our children. We have remained in contact with both of them over the past thir-ty years. Each remained true to her strengths but sadly one has also remained tied to her limitations.

One night we came home at midnight to discover her and our children huddled in a corner with all the lights out, scared to death from a noise she heard three hours earlier in the evening. For three hours she let her fears consume her. Today, at forty years old, she remains a frightened child. She never married. She lives her life in the shadows, much like we found her that evening in our home.

The other grew into a committed professional and vibrant wife and mother. She enjoys numerous relationships and refus-

In 1942, Joe Gordon lead the Major League in number of errors—he was struck out the most times and hit into the most double plays. An yet, in that same season, he won the MVP Award in the American League. Just as Joe Gordon turned the season around and became the Most Valuable Player, you, too, can overcome your faults and be recog-nized for your strengths.

es to let life challenges deny her the opportunity to enjoy an abundant life. Both came with strengths and limitations. One shied away from herself while the other evolved to become her best self.

We feel a remarkable sense of accomplishment when we see positive change in ourselves. What one person does naturally well, another may struggle to do. Some of us have emotional tempers that create havoc in our lives while others exude patience. We are here to grow through life, not simply to go through it. Learning to think and act differently is what makes life exciting and uniquely ours!

. . . .

"We have met the enemy, and he is us."
– WALT KELLY, POGO

. . . .

When I decided to engage in physical fitness more proactively, I realized that I was my greatest obstacle. Again and again it required that I face myself in order to win the day. Ultimately, getting over myself—my excuses, limitations, fears, existing (albeit unhealthy) eating patterns—was my greatest challenge. I am consistently intrigued by how much easier the process gets the longer I stay committed to getting over myself. Of course, the longer I make good choices, the less I have to fight myself making bad decisions. It all begins and continues with facing the truth about myself rather than accepting my personality limitations and negative choices.

CHAPTER SUMMARY

Points to Remember
- D + V + P > C = CHANGE
- Life is about change. Commit to proactive change in your life.
- The longer you make good choices, the less you have to fight making bad choices.

Questions to Consider
- What are you most afraid of in your life? Why?
- What life choices have you made that you should revisit and change?
- What is your vision for what you want to become as a human being?

Application Exercise #1
List the three most important personality limitations you have corrected in your life and resultant benefits.

PERSONALITY LIMITATIONS	RESULTANT BENEFITS
1) _____	1) _____
2) _____	2) _____
3) _____	3) _____

Chapter 21

Step 3: Envision Who You Want to Be

IN ORDER TO get over yourself you must have a sense of who you want to be and what you want your life to be about. Your vision must be about something greater than what you are today.

· · · · · · ·

The new vision of yourself challenges you to rise above yourself and resist the easier, less demanding route taken by most people.

· · · · · · ·

See yourself as you hope to be remembered. Are you fun? Have you traveled much? Do you give back to family and/or society? Do you physically touch people? Are you intellectually stimulating? Do you feel warm and inviting? You become what you subconsciously believe yourself capable of becoming.

Ultimately, your life is a composite of what you did, with whom you did it, why you did it, and how it made people feel. It requires constant investment of your time, effort, and resources.

You become that to which you commit. If your life is about hiding from truth or having others constantly meet your needs, so be it. If your life is about learning and stretching, becoming and giving back, such will be your legacy. In the end, you don't decide how you will be remembered. All you decide is what evidence you leave for others to determine how they will remember you.

I find myself today in the intriguing position of having to write my mother's obituary. What will I say about her life? What words best represent how she thought and what she did? In the end, our life comes down to a few simple exclamation points about who we became and how we made others feel!

Life changes, as do we. Our life vision should reflect our various stages in life. Some things remain constant while other aspects change. Align your vision with your core personality foundation, your life values, and truth. Your vision should inspire you to get over yourself and enlarge your life. A well-lived life is marked by specific moments when a person decides to take a fork in their journey, which requires overcoming something negative about themselves or something that is personally limiting.

. . . .

"Two roads diverged in a wood and I—
I took the one less traveled by,
And that has made all the difference."
– ROBERT FROST

. . . .

CHAPTER SUMMARY

Points to Remember

- *You become that to which you commit.*
- Our lives ultimately come down to a few simply exclamation points about who we became and how we made others feel!
- Life responds to you. As you change, so does your life.

Questions to Consider

- How would you be remembered if you died today?
- How do you want to be remembered in life?
- Who role-models for you a life in which he or she lives in alignment with what he or she values?

Application Exercise #1

Write a values/mission statement of at least five things you envision yourself committing to in your future. Think seriously about why you are choosing each item. Envision how your life will be enhanced by achieving each item you list. Be very specific with each commitment. Place the list somewhere that you will review it at least twice a day. (i.e. I spend 15 minutes every day reflecting on those in my life who could benefit from my attention.)

1. _____

2. _____

3. _____

4. _____

5. _____

Chapter 22

Step 4: Commit to Your Vision

YOU SEE THIRD BASE just ninety feet away. Focus on getting to third base in your life. What must you commit to that will enable you to get there safely? Keep your eye on that base and only that base. Everything else is less important right now.

. . . .

"Eighty percent of success is showing up."
– WOODY ALLEN

. . . .

I was just talking to one of my very healthy friends and reminiscing about the time when I committed to becoming physically fit. I needed a specific practical solution to give me confidence that I could commit to my long-term vision. I needed something concrete that I could do every day to be successful.

I purchased two books that became my fitness bibles. My doctor recommended *Fit for Life* by Harvey and Marilyn Diamond, which basically recommended fruits in the morning and vegetables in the afternoon, so I bought large fruit and vegetable trays and committed to my new regimen (even while traveling for business on the road!). The second book became my exercise guru, *8 Minutes in the Morning* by Jorge Cruise which basically recommended doing various exercises every morning for 8 minutes.

My friend recalls mocking me at the time saying, "8 minutes? I can't even get into my workout clothes in 8 minutes!" Obviously he exercised longer, harder, and better than I did and he couldn't relate to my *beginner mindset*. But I needed something that fit me. Today I have carved an hour out of my schedule because I discovered the power of fitness in my life, but that would never have happened earlier in my change process.

The most rewarding moments in life often come after committing to doing something and against all odds, actually achieving your goal. Once done, you often take a breather before committing to a new change or direction because maintaining focus requires tenacity and discipline. For this very reason, many people never reach third base in life.

Older people looking back admit that they most regret choosing not to risk or commit to something they knew at the time would lift their lives. Some simply took their eye off third base and remained stuck on second. Others, in telling their stories, remember starting towards their commitment but becoming distracted. Suddenly they found themselves in a pickle that got them thrown out.

Of course, one can always get back up and run the bases more successfully next time. However, some things have a time limit. If you miss them, the opportunity is gone. Take the time to envision what you want in your life and match your daily choices with your greater vision. You'll miss fewer opportunities to score.

You cannot be what you cannot see. Look at what you want your life to be about and decide if your vision is legitimate. Is the motivation behind it clean? If so, keep your eye on third base and be willing to get over yourself in order to get something more. Commit to third base!

> "...Until one is committed, there is hesitancy, the chance to draw back; always ineffectiveness. Concerning all acts of initiative (and creation), there is one elementary truth, the ignorance of which kills countless ideas and splendid plans; that the moment that one definitely commits oneself, then providence moves too.
> All sorts of things occur to help that would never otherwise have occurred. A whole stream of events issues from the decision, raising in one's favor all manner of unforeseen incidents and meetings and material assistance, which no man could have dreamt would have come his way."

> – W.H. Murray, 1951
> *The Scottish Himalayan Expedition*

Looking back at my life, I can readily see the numerous times I straddled the fence, believing I was committed when I wasn't and wondering why I failed. In EVERY situation where I have truly committed, providence moved too! That's the magic of commitment to your vision. Whatever you really want to be about, commit to it and you will discover, rather unexpectedly, success.

CHAPTER SUMMARY

Points to Remember

• "Eighty percent of success is showing up." ~ Woody Allen
• Life's most rewarding moments come after overcoming all odds and achieving your goal.
• Commit to someone or something bigger than you in order to get over yourself.

Questions to Consider

• What have you been committed to and overcome all odds to achieve in your life?
• Do you have clean motives behind your commitments and aspirations?
• Are you currently straddling the fence on a commitment that you should make?

Application Exercise #1

In getting over yourself, you must constantly do your homework. Step #5 in this process requires doing steps #1-4 with (and for) someone else in your life! Your homework for this chapter consists of helping someone else to:

(1) Accept himself and his innate gifts.
(2) Face the truth about his limited life and poor choices.
(3) Create a vision for who he wants to become in his life.
(4) Successfully commit to his vision.

Select someone you will help complete this process:

_____

Keep a record of your experience for later reflection.
I began this process on: (date)

_____

We completed this process on: (date)

_____

The benefits of assisting this person in this process were:

_____

_____

_____

_____

_____

_____

_____

_____

_____

Rounding Third Base

THIS IS WHEN we round third base and begin the final leg of our journey. We are headed home. When we learn to make our lives about others, we only legitimize ourselves. This is a very tough concept to *"get"* in life!!! Fewer get to third base than don't! You should feel triumphant in tagging third base and heading home. This base depends entirely on your ability to get over yourself. In tagging third base you demonstrated that you have developed the emotional muscle to carry someone else in life. Third base is all about becoming legitimate within yourself so you are able to devote your time, energy, and gifts to lifting others. Third base requires completing lots of homework and paying your dues.

I remember reading Scott Peck's enduring book *The Road Less Traveled,* which begins with the statement "Life is difficult." Any of us who live long enough will come to recognize the truth of this. Live long enough and you will experience heartache and disappointment, or become disillusioned, whether it is with yourself personally or with someone you love. Life is challenging. Some of our challenges we create for ourselves because we don't complete our homework or pay our dues. Some come from loving people who don't complete their homework or pay their dues.

Some of life's greatest pain is inflicted on us. It is not the pain, but how we respond to it that becomes our test. Some of life's heartache we inflict on ourselves. Getting to third base was all about learning to respond better to the challenges life throws our way AND paying our dues so we don't create needless pain for ourselves.

• What have been your greatest life challenges?
• How well have you responded to them?
• Do you respond more effectively to pain and disillusionment today than you did previously?
• How well do you prepare for life's inevitable disappointments?
• Who has created the greatest stress in your life?

Nobody runs this base path better than people who can reign in their egos and see their roles in how they respond to life's challenges. If you can get aligned with your life vision and come to terms with what is required to successfully tag third base, you will discover peace. Peace does not mean to be in a place where there is no noise, trouble, or hard work. *Peace means to be in the midst of those things and still be calm in your heart.*

Third base is all about getting aligned with first and second base. You know yourself. You know truth. Now get over yourself by aligning the two. This brings clarity. Ask yourself:

• What about your innate nature works for you in life?
• What about your innate nature works against you in life?
• Why do you deny truth and refuse to face facts in your life?
• What kind of life picture do you see when you connect the dots?
• What role have you played in creating your life picture?

You have to get past your current problems in order to move ahead in life. If you are still solving the same problems at 25 years old that you were presented with at 18, you are falling behind.

You have to correctly solve the problems life gives you before you can move on to the next level. If you are answering the wrong question or not figuring out the problems, you are holding yourself back from getting around the bases. So the ultimate question is *"What role are you playing in your life?!"*

Getting to third base is all about getting over you. It requires doing your homework and paying your dues. You must learn to value your innate gifts and value your innate self. You must be willing to face what you are doing that prevents you from being your best self. You will need others to help you here because of your natural tendency to deny, rationalize, justify, or ignore truths about yourself. You must create a positive vision for what you want your life to be about and commit to achieving your vision.

Rounding third base begins the process of getting others. You use your developed emotional strength to lift others and help them score. You learn to live without immediate gratification in order for others to experience success. You move beyond yourself to see others and what they can become.

Each base frees you to tag the next. The further you get around the bases, the more disappointing it becomes when you are stranded on base at the end of the inning. It doesn't get much more heartbreaking than being left high and dry on third base when you came so close to scoring.

You have met the challenge of tagging third base. You have the vision and the strength. Just keep your eye on where you are going. You have worked so hard to create this opportunity. It is now the final push that frees you to make life about others. Feel the freedom of no longer having to be all about you.

COMING HOME 4

Get Others

CROSSING HOME PLATE: DO WHAT FREES YOU.

. . . .

**HOME PLATE: TECHNIQUES OF
GETTING SAFELY HOME.**

. . . .

PAY ATTENTION TO OTHERS.

Chapter 23

Crossing Home Plate: What It Means to Come Home!

"In baseball the object is to go home; and to arrive safely.
I hope to arrive safely at home!"

– GEORGE CARLIN

THE YEAR WAS 1970. I still remember the day as though it was yesterday. As my plane landed in New York's JFK airport, I reflected on the past three years I had just spent traveling as an impressionable young man in Europe. The gate agent smiled and simply said, "Hi." I hadn't heard that expression "Hi" in my native tongue for three years. I was so moved just hearing it that I couldn't immediately respond. I was literally stuck in a wave of emotion that felt completely comfortable, completely right. At that very moment, I knew that I had finally come home.

Home is many things to many people. But each one of us knows inside ourselves, when we are truly home. I was reading

Dr. Jane Goodall's autobiography and felt her passion living among her apes in Africa, discovering herself to be home far from her birthplace of England.

Our personalities know when they are home as well. They know when they are comfortable and legitimate as opposed to being contrived or "acting as if." Different stages of our lives and various people in our lives do not value us being at home with ourselves nor do they promote it. We alone must demonstrate courage in accurately defining our home and protecting its integrity.

For you, home may be freedom and laughter, while others feel most at home with security and playing by the rules. The power of *The People Code* lies in its simple, telling truths about what each of our homes looks like inside. Each of us would be wise to use the book's guiding insights to design our homes so that we remain legitimate and congruent with ourselves. *It is your first responsibility to yourself and others to create an honest home for yourself where you can find comfort and truth and reassurance that you are, indeed, lovable and uniquely, legitimately you.*

Ask yourself when you were most happy, most comfortable with yourself. What activities did you engage in? Who was involved in your life? Some love new learning opportunities like taking night classes, while others enjoy outdoor sports. Some crave interaction with people and some prefer to read alone. Life is a series of *comings and goings.* We need to travel outside our comfort zones in order to enrich our lives. Before you get too caught up in your goings, get clear about your comings and create a home you can trust, from which to embark on your daily life.

· · · · · · ·

When people die, they are missed only by those whose lives they touched.

· · · · · · ·

Travel is both exciting and enlightening. I often think of the phrase, "I guess you just had to be there!" when trying to explain some of my most meaningful life adventures. And so it goes in life. We should be there—stretch and evolve and challenge ourselves to see life from different angles. I personally can't imagine life without the rich perspective I have gained from each of the personality colors. Life without a Red's gift for risk or a Blue's gift for caring or a White's gift for listening or a Yellow's gift for living in the moment would truly be limited.

But when it's all been said and done, we always come home to ourselves. We sit within ourselves like an old stuffed chair with all its ripped fabric and worn edges, comfortable in the sense that we are safe and "known" here. For all the magic of travel, being at home frees us from being strangers in a foreign land. Few would challenge Dorothy in her renowned quote from *The Wizard of Oz,* when clutching Toto under her arm, she whispered, "There's no place like home." Coming home always makes the journey more complete.

This section is about crossing home plate. The journey home is twofold. Home will always be a place we consider safe, a place that fits who we were innately born to be and the person we have chosen to become. Remember, what you choose to embrace in your life is equally who you are and what you are innately born to be. You can choose to develop attitudes and behaviors in life that were not always safe and comfortable, yet became as much a part of you as your innate self at birth.

So who are you? Do you care about helping others succeed in life or are you still caught up mostly in yourself?

If you never learn to be about others, to care about who they are and how you can help them be more successful, then you will never feel safe or comfortable crossing home plate. You will remain stuck on base when your life ends, never feeling the ultimate point of life's game: to score!

The challenge in crossing home plate lies in being true to your innate self while learning how to get others. You can not consistently get others while you are actively engaged in making life about yourself. Of all the bases, this one requires the most sacrifice, coming to an acceptance that while you do matter in life, life is not all about only you.

CHAPTER SUMMARY

Points to Remember
- It is your responsibility to create an honest home for yourself with the assurance that you are, indeed, lovable and uniquely, legitimately, you.
- When people die they are missed only by those whose lives they touched.
- Life without a Red's gift for risk, or a Blue's gift for caring, or a White's gift for listening, or a Yellow's gift for living in the moment, would truly be limited.

Questions to Consider
- When have you been most happy and comfortable with yourself? Why?
- Have you learned how to make life about others as naturally as you have made life about yourself?

• Have you disciplined yourself in learning to allow others to come first?

Application Exercise #1

List ten people who would miss you most right now in life if you were gone. Why?

NAME	RELATIONSHIP	REASON YOU'D BE MISSED
1.		
2.		
3.		
4.		
5.		
6.		
7.		
8.		
9.		
10.		

Chapter 24

Home Plate: Get Others
Techniques for Getting Safely Home

FILL IN THE blank. Who is man's best friend? _____
Of course the most common answer is "a dog." Why do so many people feel so connected to their dogs, as opposed to other people?

The simple answer is because dogs make people feel loved. They look at you and pay attention. Why do people often grandparent more effectively than they parented? They are no longer all about themselves and worrying about their perform-ances. As grandparents, all they have to do is enjoy their grand-children and pay attention to them. Typically, grandparents have moved beyond third base and are ready to "get" others.

We all know pathetic lives where age does little to ease a person's need to make life all about himself. Some grandparents still demand that a grandchild come to them on the grandpar-ents' terms. They can't hear the child because they are so busy making noise about what they want and what they need. They should learn from the dog to first meet others' needs and wants.

The reason dogs make people feel loved comes from their ability to trust. They trust that by giving, they will receive. Furthermore, they trust that in the event that they don't receive, they are secure in themselves.

. . . .

"There is no greater joy nor greater reward than to make a fundamental difference in someone's life."
– SISTER MARY ROSE MCGEADY

. . . .

THE CONCEPT OF GETTING OTHERS

Sounds so routine, so right. Yet nothing is more difficult than making life less about yourself and more about others. Despite its tragic consequences, selfishness rears its ugly head, constantly mocking us throughout the various stages of our lives. Insecurity sabotages our efforts to place the focus on others. Lack of trust that we'll "get our due" prompts us to keep raising our own flag and demanding that our own agendas be met at the expense of others. You must leave third base in order to cross home plate. In other words, you must get over making life about yourself in order to get others. And getting others challenges all of us in very different ways.

Consider the core personality color White. Of all the personality types, Whites are the most effective at accepting others and tolerating differences. They are least likely to be frustrated or irritated by others. However, as with all colors, their gift is a double-edged sword that cuts both ways. While they are most comfortable with differences, they are least comfortable with conflict and thus less likely to engage others. Similar patterns exist for each other color.

Reds are best at depersonalizing communication and speaking to the issues. They "show their cards" candidly and clearly. However, they struggle to listen to others without interrupting and in finding an empathetic connection.

Yellows are best at engaging others positively and without guile, but often suffer and are set back when they feel judged or feel negative energy coming from another person. They are more likely to move to other relationships that require less discomfort in shared interaction.

Blues naturally empathize with compassion and demonstrate a sense of genuine interest in others. They look for ways to connect with others, but struggle when others disappoint them. They often find that their judgmental nature outweighs their desire to connect when they deem another person to be inappropriate and as such, unacceptable.

So think of an individual you don't understand in your life, someone who frustrates or irritates you.

Reds and Blues will come up with more names quicker than Yellows and Whites will. However, Reds and Blues are more likely to engage in the process with someone with whom they feel disconnected than Whites or Yellows, who are more likely to simply mosey on down the road and connect with others who require less effort.

Think of the person you selected. Now ask yourself what is it ABOUT YOU that prevents you from understanding, accepting, and connecting with this individual. I promise you that the key lies in you and not in them. Often our egos get in the way. We are so busy protecting ourselves and being right that we can't see them as others do. Whites may be more accepting, less empathetic, while Blues may be more caring and less accepting. However, the answer to your relationship disconnect can most often be found inside yourself.

In order to get others you have to get over yourself. See life through other people's filters. Try and understand why they need to behave as they do. Forgiveness is often a critical element of getting others. As long as you are unable to free others from your judgment, you can never hope to see them in a clear light.

Leo Tolstoy once remarked, "Everyone wants to change the world, but no one wants to change himself." Yet, the only person you actually can change is yourself. Our world changes when we change. You hold the key to every relationship in your life. Begin by considering which color has the gift you need to embrace in order to change yourself. You will never get others unless you can first free them to be their best selves around you. What's holding you back? Ultimately you pay the price of a limited life. Life is too short to hold others hostage. Buddy Hackett once said, "While you're carrying a grudge, they're out dancing."

SIX TECHNIQUES FOR GETTING OTHERS

1. Get your ego out of the way. This is not about you. It's about creating a relationship with another person.

2. Pay attention to what the other person is doing right. You'll never see all the possibilities if you approach people in negativity.

3. Listen to what they are saying. Connect the dots to the story they are telling.

4. Listen to what they are really trying to communicate. Look behind the "what" to find the "why."

5. Free them from your judgment. It is not your job in life to determine who is worthy of your acceptance. Release yourself from the dual role of judge and jury.

6. Give them the benefit of the doubt or invite them to be their best self around you. You'll see much more of their big picture than your narrow interpretation.

Now, consider once again the person you named with whom you currently struggle. Circle each of the six techniques as you consider creating a positive connection with that individual. Be 100% responsible for making the relationship right. You will surprise yourself with how empowered you feel in getting others when you accept the six vital techniques for success in this process.

CHAPTER SUMMARY

Points to Remember
• Nothing is more difficult than making life less about yourself and more about others.
• Every personality has innate limitations that impede and strengths that enhance one's ability to get others.
• "Everyone wants to change the world, but no one wants to change himself." ~ Tolstoy

Questions to Consider

• Would people closest to you say you are more selfish or self-less? Why?

• What could you change about yourself today that would enhance someone else's life?

• Are you using forgiveness as a tool to free or imprison yourself from others?

Application Exercise #1

Name three people you could engage more effectively today. Describe what it is about you that makes you less effective with them. Explain how you will take 100% responsibility for improving the relationship.

NAME	YOUR FLAW	ACTION PLAN

1._____

2._____

3._____

Chapter 25

Pay Attention to Others

TOO SOON, OUR lives replace commas with periods and our numbered days run out. Too soon, the rich opportunities to offer assistance to others come to an end. Getting Others is an art form that often takes a lifetime to learn. It's a powerful legacy that lasts far longer than almost any other legacy we can create. The people we "got" and subsequently connected with are those for whom our life legacy continues long after we leave. They feel our loss and miss our presence.

In order to impact others, we have to value them simply because they breathe—not because of how they behave. We must grow up and stop making life about our wants and our needs. Like dogs, we must trust others to respond and know that if they don't respond positively, we have done the right thing and we are secure ourselves.

Crossing home plate takes muscle, emotionally mature muscle. It often requires commitment and sacrifice. It's all about the team scoring rather than your own personal ego. You give up so that others may receive. You eat last so that others may eat first. The happiest people always look for opportunities to understand others and help them succeed.

Karl Menninger, the renowned American psychiatrist, was asked just before he died in 1990, what he believed was the best therapy for mental illness. He said, "Lock up your house, go across the railroad tracks, find someone in need, and do something for them." Getting to third base is "locking up your house and crossing the railroad tracks." Coming home is "finding someone in need and doing something for them." Crossing home plate is all about proactively seeking opportunities to improve the living conditions of others.

This is the essence of parenting. All parents will tell you that they were most effective when they reached out to their children. Making life about others seriously enhances our own lives but for some odd reason doing so doesn't feel natural for most of us. Most of us have to learn to put others first. We have to work to keep our needs out of the equation when we are interacting with others. We are inherently selfish. Parenting is often one of the most powerful motivators for helping us get over ourselves and get others. Not always, but often, we see people emerge as heroes for their children when they would have been less likely to do it for themselves. I remember countless examples of patients who rose to a challenge on behalf of their children in ways that never would have occurred to them for themselves.

Of course, some mortal parents achieve almost immortal status with their stretch to love their children. These awesome role-models remind us mere mortals of our own potential, should we be called upon to stretch in making our lives secondary to getting others. One example is Dick and Rick Hoyt, who have mesmerized millions by their remarkable journey together. If you haven't witnessed their video, visit their website at www.teamhoyt.com for a remarkable journey of love created by a father choosing his son's happiness over his own, only to come home to a newfound life of meaning and connection in the process.

One of my own life heroes is the perhaps all time greatest college basketball coach, John Wooden, whose phenomenal record speaks for itself. He once said, "You can't live a perfect day without doing something for someone who will never be able to repay you."

We must meet our children where they are and join them in their world rather than expect them to meet us in our own. Selfish parents are unable to go the distance to their children while selfless parents find ways to make life about those they brought into the world, enhancing their lives with every opportunity. This is what gets you across home plate and creates winning strategies for life.

I was recently discussing marriage with a husband and wife who were about to celebrate their fortieth wedding anniversary. He has never loved her effectively. In stretching to save the marriage, he has revisited interrupting her in conversation, pouting, and a multitude of other negative behaviors. In other words he has stopped acting negatively in the relationship. However, he has done nothing proactive to improve the marriage. He has stepped up his game considerably on the defense but he is doing nothing to score points on the offense. YOU CAN'T WIN UNLESS YOU SCORE!

Crossing home plate is playing offense. You have to be proactive to score! You can't be proactive if you aren't paying attention to what others are all about. Yet, it doesn't make much sense to go to all the effort to get stranded on third base.

I see this in business all of the time also. Young employees looking to move up in the company often forget to pay attention to what their boss is all about. They get so caught up in themselves that they forget to "get their boss," the very person who will make all the difference in their career development.

They keep wondering why they get passed over for promotion but never consider that perhaps what their employer is looking for is very different from what they exude.

We need to wake up and pay attention to those whom we value. And the more people we can value simply because they exist, the greater capacity we have to score more often in life. We need to be willing to commit and ready to sacrifice our own personal agendas if we ever hope to cross home plate. At the end of the day, it's not about you. The well-lived life is about serving others, serving their wants and needs, understanding their fears and hopes, making them successful in life.

In some strange way, lifting others frees you to drive your own life abundantly. Just one of those amazing mysteries of life. Like the following story that will stay with you long after you have placed this book back on your bookshelf, it's a reminder of how we must be proactive in our service to others. We must score points by seeing what others need if we ever hope to play life to win. Please note that the story has been widely circulated on the internet and through email, which is how I came across it. The original story was titled "Perfection at the Plate," and can be found in Echoes of the Maggid, by Rabbi Paysach Krohn (Mesorah Publications, 1999).

At a fundraising dinner for a school that serves learning disabled children, the father of one of the students delivered a speech that would never be forgotten by any who attended. After extolling the school and its dedicated staff, he offered a question.

"When not interfered with by outside influences, everything nature does is done with perfection. Yet my son, Shay, cannot learn things as other children do. He cannot understand things as other children do. Where is the natural order of things in my son?"

The audience was stilled by the query.

The father continued. "I believe, that when a child like Shay comes into the world, an opportunity to realize true human nature presents itself, and it comes, in the way other people treat that child."

Then he told the following story: Shay and his father had walked past a park where some boys Shay knew were playing baseball.

Shay asked, "Do you think they'll let me play?"

Shay's father knew that most of the boys would not want someone like Shay on their team, but the father also understood that if his son were allowed to play, it would give him a much-needed sense of belonging. Shay's father approached one of the boys on the field and asked if Shay could play.

The boy looked around for guidance and, getting none, he took matters into his own hands and said, "We're losing by six runs and the game is in the eighth inning. I guess he can be on our team and we'll try to put him in to bat in the ninth inning."

In the bottom of the eighth inning, Shay's team scored a few runs but was still behind by three. In the top of the ninth inning, Shay put on a glove and played in the outfield. Even though no hits came his way, he was obviously ecstatic just to be in the game and on the field, grinning from ear to ear as his father waved to him from the stands.

In the bottom of the ninth inning, Shay's team scored again. Now, with two outs and the bases loaded, the potential winning run was on base and Shay was scheduled to be next at bat.

At this juncture, should they let Shay bat and give away their chance to win the game? Surprisingly, Shay was given the bat. Everyone knew that a hit was all but impossible because Shay didn't even know how to hold the bat properly, much less connect with the ball.

However, as Shay stepped up to the plate, the pitcher moved

in a few steps to lob the ball in softly so Shay could at least be able to make contact. The first pitch came and Shay swung clumsily and missed. The pitcher again took a few steps forward to toss the ball softly towards Shay. As the pitch came in, Shay swung at the ball and hit a slow ground ball right back to the pitcher. The pitcher picked up the soft grounder and could have easily thrown the ball to the first baseman. Shay would have been out and that would have been the end of the game.

Instead, the pitcher took the ball and turned and threw it on a high arc to right field, far beyond the reach of the first baseman. Everyone started yelling, "Shay, run to first! Run to first!" Never in his life had Shay ever made it to first base. He scampered down the baseline, wide-eyed and startled. Everyone yelled, "Run to second! Run to second!"

By the time Shay rounded first base, the right fielder had the ball. He could have thrown the ball to the second-baseman for the tag, but he understood the pitcher's intentions and intentionally threw the ball high and far over the third-baseman's head. Shay ran toward second base as the runners ahead of him circled the bases toward home. Shay reached second base, the opposing shortstop ran to him, turned him in the direction of third base, and shouted, "Run to third!" As Shay rounded third, the boys from both teams were screaming, "Shay, run home!" Shay ran to home, stepped on the plate, and was cheered as the hero who hit the "grand slam" and won the game for his team.

"That day," said the father softly with tears now rolling down his face, "the boys from both teams helped bring a piece of true love and humanity into this world."

If you had been the pitcher, what would you have done?

About the Author

DR. TAYLOR HARTMAN is recognized around the world for his dynamic contributions in the field of psychology. He has written three bestselling non-fiction books. *The People Code* was followed by *Color Your Future*, and *Sandcastles: The Art of Loving for All Kinds of Relationships*. He consults and lectures with businesses and provides personal coaching for select individuals. He and his wife, Jean, have five children and seven grandchildren. They live in Salt Lake City.

For more information, visit www.taylorhartman.com.